Scribe Publications
FAULTLINES

George Megalogenis spent eleven years in the Canberra press gallery, from 1988 to 1999, before moving to Melbourne as a senior feature writer for the *Australian* covering national affairs. During federal election campaigns he writes a daily column for the paper. He has a degree in economics from the University of Melbourne, and lives in Melbourne.

For Nicola and Thomas

FAULT LINES

race, work, and the politics of changing Australia

George Megalogenis

Scribe Publications
Melbourne

Scribe Publications Pty Ltd
PO Box 523
Carlton North, Victoria, Australia 3054
Email: scribe@bigpond.net.au

First published by Scribe Publications 2003

Edited by Vanessa Russell
Typeset in 11.5/16pt Stempel Garamond by the publisher
Printed and bound in Australia by Griffin Press

National Library of Australia
Cataloguing-in-Publication data

Megalogenis, George.
Faultlines : race, work, and the politics of changing Australia.

ISBN 1 920769 05 6.

1. Equality - Australia. 2. Social justice - Australia. 3. Australia - Social conditions. I. Title.

300.994

www.scribepub.com.au

Contents

Acknowledgements

I wrote the bulk of this book on holidays, so the people I am most indebted to are my nephew and niece for tolerating their uncle's absences over the summer of 2002–3, when we should have been at the beach.

At the end of June 2003, I figured I should take a real holiday, but Henry Rosenbloom at Scribe sought to foil that plan when he called on the Monday, day one of my five-day break, to say that the very rough manuscript I'd sent him that weekend was worth persisting with. His prompt two-day reply, and Russ Radcliffe's enthusiasm in accepting my call, would put many of the dear friends I have in the newspaper game to shame. Thank you, Henry and Russ. Also to Vanessa Russell for her thoughtful edit: this book is the better for your input. And full respect to Matthew Kelly, who had the decency, after reading an early sample of my work, to suggest Scribe as the vehicle for it — now that's capitalism with a human face.

There are too many colleagues at the *Australian* to name, and in any case I'm bound to forget one, so I'll show my appreciation with a beer or three to each when we next meet. But the freedom they gave me to roam across the political and economic landscapes yielded the scoops, published first in our national broadsheet, that are at the heart of this book. Thank you to everyone who assisted with those stories: journalists, political contacts, and the ex-students of Ringwood High School for their time in August 2001, and again two years later in agreeing to have their words reproduced here.

Thanks also to the public affairs and client services departments at the Australian Bureau of Statistics for responding so patiently to my nit-picking requests.

To Bill Leak, whose genius is sprinkled throughout this book, you have my life-long appreciation for taking the time to translate my words into pictures. If the words fall short, at least we have some brilliant cartoons to show people that there is a story here worth telling.

Last, and of course, most importantly, thanks to the friends and family who — like Bill, Henry, Russ, Vanessa, and Matthew — indulged me on this project by letting me talk about it and helping me sharpen the manuscript. In alphabetical order they are: Gabrielle Chan, Bronwen Colman, Joel Deane, Margaret Easterbrook, Anna Ferguson, Joe Fulco, Marie-Claire Gateaux, Geoff Ginn, Fiona Hando, Jeff Jenkins, Anne McCaig, Richard Paddington, Jo Setright, Allison Sloan, and Anna Ziaras. Finally, I want to thank Nicola, for interviewing her grandmother for chapter one, and Thomas, for lending me his decade-old Apple Mac for the first draft.

Introduction

WHO ARE WE? In August 2001, just two months prior to an election he feared might be lost, John Howard turned away a boatload of asylum-seekers. It was this act that transformed him from the underdog into the most dominant politician of his era. Howard received three cheers from old Australia, and won a third term in office.

August 2001 was also the month in which the national census was collected. It revealed an Australia that was becoming more feminine and more cosmopolitan at its core. Women now formed the majority of the professional workforce. Also, new mothers were returning to their jobs quicker than ever. To complete the picture of new Australia, Asians — the immigrants that the right warned we could not absorb — now numbered almost one in five in the Prime Minister's electorate of Bennelong, in Sydney's comfortable and relaxed inner north.[1]

So how can Australia be both an open immigrant society, and a nation that closes its doors to refugees fleeing dictatorships in Afghanistan and Iraq? An economy that favours women, but with a political and business superstructure that is run by men? A federal parliament where the middle class is the new outcast because it voted with the opposition at the last election? To understand these dichotomies, we need to know the people of our future who will decide how Australia will develop. These people are the university-educated daughters of old Australia, and the sons and daughters of the immigrants of new Australia. Together, they are redefining the nation's middle class, and repositioning it from the old suburban quarter-acre blocks to new inner-city apartments. But our political system does not yet know how to engage these people, or even what to call them.

I could dub the Generation X women and the local-born children of post-war immigrants as, simply, 'women' and 'wogs'. As a Greek–Australian and a journalist, I have found that I can use the word 'wog' in print. But this word still offends more people than it empowers, so I will use it sparingly. Instead, we need a concept to unite the two groups. So let's employ 'Generation W'.

This is the generation that is best suited to the demands of our open-all-hours economy. But there is a catch. Prosperity has also given it the licence to snub politics, which is why this new middle class has yet to achieve true influence in government. The electoral cycle will, however, be forced to catch up with Generation W and deliver a prime minister from within its ranks. Only it won't feel like a social revolution. By then, Australia will be a decidedly less 'macho' place. Voters won't notice a woman or the offspring of a non-English-speaking immigrant in the Lodge, any more than they did the first Catholic prime minister. That's how Australia works: its politicians tend to lag behind the community by a few years. Of course, Generation W may produce equally aloof leaders to match the current crop of politicians. That's why we need to know its constituents as they live today, in the real world. I will do this by getting beneath the unpublished figures of the August 2001 census and giving a taste of what is to come. I will also reveal the secret opinion polling conducted by the main political parties to explain what voters really think about the debates on national identity: from reconciliation, to refugees, to the war in Iraq. This book tells two stories — one optimistic, the other painful — about the people and politics of new and old Australia.

⁂ ⁂ ⁂

Leadership has become the punchline to a national joke. The further one climbs the political or corporate ladder in Australia, the greater the risk of being held up to public ridicule. The tall-poppy syndrome is no longer the explanation. In the new millennium, what sets apart leaders from citizens is that leaders are no longer accountable in the truest sense of the word. The distance from our leaders is compounded by an act of mutually assured cynicism: we ignore them, allowing many to remain in power way past their welcome. Public apathy becomes the politicians' shield, which allows them to use public opinion to disempower their voters.

The process starts with the highest office in the land, the one office that is supposed to be above politics. As governor-general, Peter Hollingworth managed to unite Australians against him. His handling of child sex-abuse cases in his previous job as Anglican archbishop of Brisbane also tainted the church. It was a farce of Pythonesque proportions. Hollingworth clung to his taxpayer-funded post for more than a year after the scandal became public. Finally, in mid-2003, he resigned, some fifteen months after the first opinion poll had found that almost two out of three voters wanted him gone.[2]

At the same time, the nation's indigenous lobby was run by an alleged sex offender. As chairman of the Aboriginal and Torres Strait Islander Commission, Geoff Clark managed to jell left and right against him. He refused repeated calls to stand aside from his taxpayer-funded post pending the outcome of a civil trial for rape.

At the top end of town, business operated on the principle that executives should be paid a bonus for each fall in the share price. As head of AMP, George Trumbull made the electorate so angry that it named him, unprompted, in focus-group discussions held by the main political parties at the start of the new millennium. In 1999, Trumbull pocketed a $13 million payout, despite being pushed out of AMP after overseeing a doomed takeover of fellow insurer GIO. Somehow, the message did not get through to other company chiefs, who awarded themselves even bigger packages when their companies went bankrupt — leaving staff, shareholders, and creditors empty-handed. Today, the names One.Tel and HIH are triggers for community anger.

The era's dissonance is embodied by its most successful politician, John Howard. The Prime Minister found that the key to victory at the ballot box was to harness issues that divided people: the three Rs of republic, reconciliation, and refugees. These arguments pitted new Australia against old Australia, city versus bush, and inner city versus the rest of the nation. At the 2001 election, Howard didn't need the consent of the middle class to prevail. His coalition government achieved majorities in both the top and bottom 50 federal electorates, as ranked by family income. But the middle 50 seats went the other way.[3]

Those who are pro-republic, pro-reconciliation, and pro-refugees see the failure of these agendas as a sign that Australia is reactionary at heart. The conservatives, on the other hand, see rejection of the three Rs as an affirmation of a nation that eschews elitism. Both arguments are flawed. The mistake that the pessimistic left and the pre-eminent right makes is to assume that these issues have been settled in the negative, and that the public can't be bothered facing them anymore. Debate will resume when Howard departs. The next Liberal leader will not be able to ignore the nation's centre, because the bottom 50 seats will inch back to Labor. In any case, it does not follow that the public's lack of interest in the three Rs equals the acceptance of monarchy, third world living standards endured by Australian Aboriginals, or the tactics employed in the war on boat people.

The end of political correctness is a prime boast of the Howard government. It's time to take the Prime Minister at his word and discuss the once-taboo topics of race and sex from the perspectives of both ends of Australia, new and old. This will help us find where the nation is moving to, beyond the fog of politics. At the heart of this narrative is a tussle as old as Adam and Eve. For Generation W to fulfil its potential, it needs to get over two character flaws of old Australia: xenophobia and sexism.

THERE MUST BE A NASTY WOG IN THE AIR...
AHCHOO!
Bill Leak

CHAPTER ONE

Generation W

'It will once again be possible to debate sensitive issues in this country without being accused of being a racist, or an extremist, or a bigot.'
—John Howard, speech, May 1996

THERE ARE THREE PHASES of wogdom: cowed, cocky, and connected. Get to the third phase and you can lose that ethnic chip on your shoulder. It doesn't matter who calls you 'wog' after that because you no longer question your identity as an Australian.

In December 2000, a supporter of Pauline Hanson took scissors to one of my columns for the *Australian* newspaper and mailed the cutting back to me. My paragraph criticising Hanson, the then leader of the One Nation Party, had a cross drawn through it, and the sentence that spelt out her offending quote had a tick. A small, precise tear ran through Bill Leak's cartoon of my swarthy head. Beside it, the reader wrote: 'WOG DOG DAGO ARSE. HOLE. A FACE LIKE A MISSHAPEN CUNT.' It was the first occasion I had been called a wog in ages. It was also the first time an adult had said it to my face, albeit only a drawing of it. The word 'wog' hurt as a child; it ripped through me like a tracer bullet. I took it personally then. In the new millennium, it said more about its author, and the politician he or she identified with, than it did about me.

My initial memories of my first phase of wogdom are not of being made to feel like olive trash — that came later. Life, as I recall it, took shape innocently enough in 1969, when I was five. It was the year of the moon landing. The year I hurled a rock at a friend for fun; which missed, and left a crater in my mother's forehead. The year of the first Richmond Tigers' premiership I cared about. Why the Tigers? My mother had landed in Australia seven years earlier, in 1962, aged twenty. She had no family here. A woman from her parents' village gave her a place to stay above a fish 'n' chip shop in Victoria Street, Richmond, in the inner city of Melbourne. This was the suburb she referred back to when she picked a football team for my sister and me to follow. Mum saw Australian Rules football as a part of life in her new home and didn't want her children to miss out. Fortunately, my father, a follower of the now-extinct Fitzroy Lions, did not have a say in our brainwashing.

My sister's seven-year-old daughter once asked her grandmother why she came to Australia. She replied, 'We were four sisters in Greece, and we were poor. I came here for a better life'. On arrival, my mother shared two rooms with eight other Greek girls. Every morning the fish 'n' chip proprietor took her young charges to local factories for job interviews. At one point in the 1970s, Mum's siblings dotted the globe. Her eldest sister, also a factory worker, lived in Germany. Her youngest sister, a teacher, was in Zambia. Her kid brother was in Germany studying to be a surgeon. Only the fourth sister never left; she stayed in the village they grew up in, Nestorio, in the northern province of Kastoria. Today, my mother is the only foreigner. The rest have returned to Greece. And Richmond, the most ironic team in the Australian Football League, which wins and loses when it is not meant to, is still messing with her head.

I learned the word 'wog' when I changed primary schools in 1972. That was the year that stung. The year I felt isolation before my time. The year the Tigers gave me my first case of heartbreak when they were raging favourites but capitulated in the grand final.

I spent the best part of the last Saturday in September 1974 perched halfway up the tree that blanketed the front of our house in North Caulfield, a few kilometres south-east of Melbourne's CBD. My gangly ten-year-old world collapsed as I climbed, branch in one hand, Philips transistor in the other. Richmond, playing in its third straight grand final, had just surrendered the lead to North Melbourne, now known only as the Kangaroos. That tree offered not only shelter from my clan, who were loudly going mad in the kitchen; it also gave me space to plan for what lay ahead. Being one of the least popular kids at school, and a wog to boot, I knew a kicking awaited me if we lost. Anyone who didn't follow the yellow and black that day wanted the 'Roos to win their first flag. Fortunately, Richmond scored the next goal, a sure sign from above that I had changed our luck by shifting lairs.

However, an hour later, with victory sealed, my melancholy returned. I couldn't gloat like the previous year, when the Tigers achieved sweet retribution against unloved Carlton. The boy braggart in me was finally quelled after two-and-a-bit years of being told I was a wog. As silly as it seems today, when I was young I thought that I wasn't a real person. That's what being a wog in a very 'white' school felt like. I was tall, but not a tough kid, so the shorter toughs in the schoolyard saw me as easy prey. My previous schoolmates, in nearby East Malvern, had been rougher, but they didn't have any reason to take it out on me. The street I grew up in had more Greek than Australian families in it. At age five, six, and seven, I felt like one of the class. At eight, nine, and ten, I was an outcast.

I was in the victim's pickle: a sensitive Greek–Australian boy without the social tools to deflect the barbs. For a while, I tilted at the taunts, like a Wog Quixote. Dumb move. That's when the beltings started. I still cringe at the word I threw at a Jewish boy in reply to the sticks 'n' stones and words he cast at me. I didn't know what it meant, but I'd heard another boy hurl it, and saw that it struck a nerve. Funnily enough, I never had anything smarter to say to the Aussie boys than to call them stupid. Truth wasn't a good defence then. It just earned you another thumping. I never hit back, which is more than many of my age can say. Taking the blows was a tactic to end the rumbles — and to avoid the principal, a man who looked and sounded like the menacing Penguin in the 'Batman' television series. Having worn the strap in 1973 for a trivial infringement — kissing a girl — I reasoned that a race riot of 20 against one would end in my expulsion. Incidentally, my fair-skinned, blue-eyed younger sister does not recall being called a wog.

⁂

Generation W, the Australian-born children of post-war immigrants, were raised to break with the past. Our parents insisted we do well at school so that we wouldn't descend to the dead-end jobs that would stop us from becoming Australians. Yet the harder we tried in class, the harsher the recriminations at recess. In those days, we wore two kick-me signs: 'wog' and 'square'. Nevertheless, our playground always found a new target. All I had to do was learn to close my mouth before it got smacked. This is how shit-stirrers are schooled; a necessary grounding for reporting national politics, I figured later.

The boy who took my place was a refugee from Chile. His family had fled from Augusto Pinochet and his butchers. His name was Adolf. I can't recall if it ended with an 'f' or a 'ph'; either way, he was stuffed. I stuck up for Adolf: an alliance of misfits. His mouth was as big as mine had been, but English was his second language. One day, a school bully, a Catholic boy, ran away from home. On his return, Adolf ribbed him that the police were going to get him. We wouldn't have known then that 'police' to Adolf meant 'death squad'. I don't know what happened to Adolf. He changed schools soon after. What he taught me, though, was how quickly Australians adapt to foreign faces. All they needed was someone else to pick on. Adolf made it easier for me because he was less familiar to my classmates. It is the most frustrating part of the Australian compact: immigrants are only accepted in hindsight after the next intake arrives.

The first of the Indo-Chinese boat people began landing in 1976. Suddenly, we wogs were not so alien. Olive trash would soon morph into olive chic. At high school, at university, and at work, Greek parents were a ticket to hipdom. We called ourselves 'wogs'. It was the second phase of wogdom, and it took place in the late 1970s and early 1980s, when you could greet an Anglo-Celt with the putdown of 'skippy' and know he wouldn't dare call you 'wog' in return. From time to time I still lie to my friends that I am a direct descendant of Ulysses, the ancient king of my father's birthplace of Ithaca. The w-word they give me in reply has twice as many letters as wog.

The third phase of wogdom occurs when you are happily Australian. However, not everyone wants to get there. *The Wog Boy*, a box-office hit in 2000, was not a bad film. But it wasn't a good one either. The best gag was from the Serbo-Croatian hit man who said he awoke every morning with the urge to kill himself. The movie missed the point because it celebrated the second phase of wogdom. It was a dated indicator of Greek–Australian inclusion that we had already surpassed. The wog boy today isn't pulling chicks and dole cheques. He is a wog in work. The mass-marketed picture we really need to see in the new millennium is *The Chink Boy*, *The Boong Boy*, or *The Leb Boy*. But we'd be too politically correct for that, right?

That's the point. The regular movie-goer will only embrace an ethnic piss-take during the third phase of wogdom, by which time its subjects have moved on and no longer need to call themselves wogs.

A former colleague in the federal parliamentary press gallery once made us laugh when he repeated a story from his Sydney mother. 'Asians have moved into our streets', he announced. He wasn't joking. It bothered him, which was why the rest of us were amused. He should have taken the train to my parents' home in Melbourne. It passes through South Yarra, the stop for Melbourne Boys High. I was commuting after 3.00 p.m. one day when the carriages were overrun by the dirty grey uniform of my youth. What struck me was not that I had been a lout like them — that was not news — but the number of Asian–Australian faces in that tornado of testosterone. They seemed comfortable and relaxed in their own skins, in the way that I had been at the same age. Almost seamlessly, they had joined Generation W.

What these boys would not know is that in the early 1980s, the graffiti that some young angry men carved into their desks at Melbourne Boys High was 'KILL GOOKS'. These Anglo-Celts were not popular. In fact, they were a bit on the scary side. As for their Vietnamese targets, well, we didn't have any in our school at the time, so the barbs were lost on them.

* * *

The women of new Australia share a kinship with new Australians. Just as they leapfrogged their mothers by making it to university, we, the Australian-born children of immigrants, also exceeded the qualifications and, thus, met the expectations, of our parents. Our mothers and fathers, children of World War II, were lucky to have completed primary school before migrating to Australia. Our experience is something old Australia can appreciate through the eyes of its own daughters.

Women have taken over the most important section of the labour market, the fulcrum of a clever nation. At the August 2001 census, they formed the majority (53 per cent) of the nation's 1.5 million professional workers. Women also secured almost two out of three (62 per cent) of the 710,000 tertiary degrees awarded between 1991 and 2001. They became the reinforcements that will soon cement the shift from a male to a female economy.[1] On its own, this would be big news. When combined with the ascension of the children of immigrants, it spells social revolution.

The potency of Generation W was confirmed, ironically, by immigration sceptics in the Howard government. In May 2002, the government released a study called, 'Second Generation Australians', which compared qualifications and incomes of the Australian-born children of immigrants with those of 'white' Australia. The expert panel included Dr Bob Birrell, of Monash University, a critic of multiculturalism. They reported these findings:

- Olive- and yellow-skinned members of Generation W, or what the reports terms 'second generation Australians', are more successful than all others of their age group:

> Those whose parents arrived in Australia in the post-war years have achieved better educational and occupational outcomes than those with Australian-born parents. The study also found the second generation of people from Southern and Eastern Europe and Asia had a higher proportion of people with university qualifications and in professional occupations than the second generation whose parents migrated from the United Kingdom or other Western European countries.

- We shouldn't wince at immigrants who can't speak English, because their children are likely to be doing better:

> Almost all second generation youth are proficient in English regardless of their parents' level of English competency. This should help in their integration into Australian society and the labour market.

- You have a greater chance of being left behind in new Australia if your lower-income parents are 'white' and were born here, than if they came by boat from, say, Vietnam:

> Second generation youth from lower socio-economic backgrounds may have a greater capacity to overcome their disadvantage than their third generation peers by participating longer in education and obtaining post-school qualifications.[2]

In immigration, it helps if your parents feel they have something to prove. This is why, on average, Generation W outperformed not just the Australian-born of Australian-born parents — eclipsing the third generation is an iron law of human nature — but also exceeded the 'white' second generation, the children of English-speaking immigrants who felt more at home growing up here. This is the mojo that drives a progressive nation: the desire of new arrivals to give themselves and their children a better life.

The finding that Generation W is better educated and wealthier, on average, than 'white' Australia should assure us that immigration is working. Yet this also contains the seed of the nation's angst, and explains why new and old Australia don't see eye to eye at the moment. Generation W are the 'it' people of globalisation, the ones who have been most able to adapt to the rigours of a deregulated economy. The person most likely to feel alienated by Generation W's triumph is the man of old

Australia, the one who saw the job-for-life economy crumble during his lifetime. Generation W, for its part, does not relate to the blue-collar male because he doesn't live amongst the working women and immigrants of the inner cities. This is not to take sides, but to acknowledge the obvious. The essence of the nation's current identity crisis is that new and old Australia don't know each other. What we are seeing is not a repeat of the generation gap of the 1960s between conservative middle-class fathers and their sons and daughters, but instead a separation of Australia by postcode: one version exists predominately in the inner city, at odds with the other, spread across the outer suburbs and country towns. These clans have no familial ties. Each views the other as an alien, an abomination of their version of Australia.

A search of the unconscious of the male old Australian shows how he sees women and immigrants as two parts of his dispossession. Thus, when the angry 'white' male reaches for a race sledge, he tends to merge it with misogyny. The pairing of colour and a pejorative for a woman's vagina earned Australian cricketer Darren Lehmann a five-match suspension in the summer of 2002–3, when he called his Sri Lankan opponents 'black cunts'. There is another connection between immigrant and woman that is more primal still: the local boy fearing foreign competition. It is said that Adolf Hitler gave racism a bad name. But he had one thing in common with the lynch mobs of the old American south who worried about the black man seducing their innocent maidens. In *Mein Kampf*, Hitler wrote:

> With satanic joy in his face, the black-haired Jewish youth lurks in wait for the unsuspecting girl whom he defiles with his blood, thus stealing her from her people. With every means he seeks to destroy the racial foundations of the people he has set out to subjugate.[3]

Our Australian men also worried about foreign competition during World War II, although it was a 'white' ally that troubled them. The US soldiers stationed in Brisbane were envied because of their fatter pay packets and success with local girls. On 26 November 1942, a scuffle between three tipsy Australian soldiers and a US private quickly mutated into a riot involving several hundred people. The Battle of Brisbane, as it was dubbed, ended with one Australian shot dead and nineteen injured on both sides. It was an ethnic gang brawl by another name, fuelled by two basic elements of xenophobia: sex and money. As US sergeant Bill Bentson recalled 60 years later:

> Walking down the street, some Aussie would say: 'There's another Yank with one of our girls'. I've never run so fast because I could see what they were doing.[4]

History, as Karl Marx once said, repeats: first as tragedy, second as farce. The politics of sex and race fused again in the new millennium as the media became obsessed over a series of pack rapes in south-west Sydney. When it became apparent that a gang of Lebanese–Australian boys had deliberately targeted 'white' Australian women, it proved to be an incendiary story. It remains a highly sensitive topic. Let's not delude ourselves: these crimes were a calculated act of racism. Often the r-word is used too liberally in the race debate in Australia. But it applies here, because these rapes were motivated by the two central tenets of racism: an assumption of superiority by one group, and their attempt to subjugate a racial 'other'. One of the themes of this book is what these brutal attacks triggered in the rest of the nation. The response was xenophobic because it involved, literally, a fear of strangers. The impulse is very Australian and dates back to the first fleet.

⁂ ⁂ ⁂

The slur of 'ethnic gang' is one of the most disturbing aspects of the first phase of wogdom. The initial boat people were, of course, British. The majority of the first fleet convicts, 'around 440 of the 736' were Londoners.[5] The first ethnic gang, though, was Irish. The illegal bookmaker John Wren, who ran the side streets and back lanes of Collingwood in inner-city Melbourne between World Wars I and II, was the prototype of the ethnic crook who tainted a community. The media he attracted in his day left the impression that his activities were something only his people would contemplate — proof, in fact, that the Irish were unlawful, underhanded, and un-Australian.

On 22 August 2001, just five days before the *Tampa* sailed into the headlines, the *Daily Telegraph* said it would be 'wrong not to address an issue as serious as gang rape by one sector of the community because it may offend an ethnic group'. The editorial is a case study of misconception. By attaching a cultural motive to the crimes, it assumed they could have been prevented by ethnic figureheads:

> Leaders of these communities have a responsibility to encourage members to observe the laws of this country and assist in assimilation of their former countrymen in their adopted home ... Under multicultural policies, migrants are free to practise their religion and customs. It is a practice in which most Australians take great pride because of the success and benefits such cultural diversity has brought this country. In return, co-operation is expected when the law is broken. The only contribution of these leaders so far has been attempts to shift responsibility from their communities.[6]

What would this newspaper have thought if the subject had

been the Port Arthur massacre in 1996? Would the editorial writer have said: 'Leaders of the Tasmanian community have a responsibility to encourage lone "white" males such as Martin Bryant to observe the laws of this country'?

Italian–Australians wore the communal jibe of 'mafia' up until the 1970s. The very first edition of the *Australian*, published on 15 July 1964, carried a seven-paragraph report on its front page:

> MAFIA ATTACK ALLEGED
>
> A 46-year-old Italian migrant yesterday said he was kicked and punched insensible by three members of the Sicilian terrorist organisation, the Mafia. Mr John Dellacosta of Lewis Drive, Figtree, a suburb of Wollongong, said [he] was viciously attacked on July 4 after he had refused demands for chickens and vegetables from his two-acre property.[7]

There is still a mafia of sorts operating today — it usually makes headlines when one Melbourne gangland figure kills another in his home, and then he, in turn, is executed at the local footy ground.[8] But the mafia no longer scares as an ethnic gang. In the 1980s and 1990s the mafia was replaced in the nation's mind by the Asian triads who have now stood aside for Lebanese gangs.

There is still no hard evidence that the Lebanese-born, or their Australian-born children, are more prone to crime than other new arrivals. In fact, the Australian Bureau of Statistics prisoners' survey for 30 June 2001 shows that the Lebanese-born barely make it into the top ten. Australian Aboriginals suffer the highest imprisonment rate. For indigenous men, the figure is almost 22 times greater than for all other Australian-born adults. Second are the Romanian-born, who are three times more likely to be in jail than the Australian-born. Then come

Vietnamese, Indonesians, Laotians, Fijians, Papua New Guineans, Cambodians, and Turks. Frightened yet? The Lebanese-born are tenth, with a mere 1.88 per 1000 in prison, just ahead of New Zealanders on 1.76 per 1000, and not that far in front of the Australian-born, who are on 1.59 for every 1000.[9]

The ethnic gang stigma inevitably leaves when a new immigrant menace is found. The fact that Australian-born boys committed the gang rapes complicates the debate for some, but doesn't alter the larger demographic forces at play. The majority of Lebanese–Australians are no different to the majority of 'white' Australians generally: they are not found in jails, but in jobs. The double standard of the left was to deny that these gang rapists hated 'white' women. The blunder of the right was to allow these crimes to reflect on an entire community.

It all depends on which phase of wogdom you are in. New arrivals are not allowed the presumption of innocence: that they are people, with a roughly similar mix of the brilliant, the bland, and the bad as anyone else. Or, as American writer Hunter S. Thompson put it more succinctly and sarcastically:

> My prejudice is pretty general, far too broad and sweeping for any racial limitations. It's clear to me — and has been since the age of ten or so — that most people are bastards, thieves and, yes, even pigfuckers. There are not many good people in this world.[10]

Australians are a contrary folk. Once you have moved into the third phase of wogdom and have passed your immigrant initiation, the pendulum of prejudice swings to an equally surreal place where even the ethnic 'spiv' can become a star. The welfare bludger in *The Wog Boy* taps a rich vein of pop-culture hypocrisy in which a rorter — or worse — can become a dysfunctional hero. Tony Soprano of 'The Sopranos' is the postmodern version in the United States, and many of us can recite lines from the *Godfather* movies. But we have to learn to love immigrants before we can lionise them. This, of course, is not to suggest that we will one day find mirth in gang rape. Rather, we will be prepared to relate to a Leb boy on commercial television who fancies himself more than women fancy him. We will indulge him in his tongue-in-cheek delusions, just as we did the self-styled stud in *The Wog Boy.*[11]

In sport, we already have a Muslim Leb boy to be awed by. Hasem el Masri is a rugby league hero who can kick goals blindfolded from most parts of the park. El Masri's exploits for the Canterbury–Bankstown Bulldogs don't prove that all Lebanese–Australians are superior athletes, any more than the misfits in the community prove that they are all rapists. It is simply easier to treat the ordinary people in between as human beings once we get to know one of their over-achievers. However much it may seem that Australia has regressed, the anti-Islam noise of the new millennium is not that different to what came before it. Yes, the gang rapes were appalling; but, no, they shouldn't stop Generation W from adding Muslims to its ranks before the end of this decade. Interestingly, on one level the Bali bombings of October 2002 proved to be less divisive than the gang rapes, because Australians were by now making an effort to distinguish the fanatics from mainstream Muslims.

History is on Australia's side. Previous immigration waves, from southern Europe, then from Asia, suffered the same initiation as those of Islamic faith today. Each group was seen as one ethnicity too many in our melting pot. Each group proved the pessimists wrong. Australians underestimate the power of their national brand. We fear that our relative youth as a settled 'white' nation means we can't compete with the thousands of years of history that other parts of the world have. That's why we always worry about the next intake being the nut we can't crack — the immigrants who will rob and rape us. We forget that what makes Australia work is that we represent the new world: the place that offers immigrants the chance to shed the cultural baggage of the old world. They want to be more like us than we realise; otherwise, why would they come here?

Immigration is one of the keys to an independent national identity. Almost a century before the *Tampa,* Irish-Catholics were attacked as traitors for arguing against conscription during World War I. They happened to be on the winning side of that debate. Their stand was vindicated, not only at consecutive referenda held in 1916 and 1917, but also in the way Australia generally looks back at that period. Gallipoli is seen as a symbol of unity — not, as it was then, a flashpoint for sectarianism. Yet at many pro-conscription rallies at the time a resolution was passed that makes the more recent race cards played by politicians seem G-rated by comparison:

> That this meeting of loyal citizens view with grave concern the disloyal and seditious utterances of prelates of the Roman Catholic Church, especially at a time when the whole of the liberties of our Empire are at stake. It urges the Commonwealth Government to take action without respect of persons to repress all such treasonable utterances.[12]

The idea that new arrivals take their orders from a foreign church and refuse to conform to Australian values is as old as sectarianism, the mafia, and the triads. The two conscription referenda also demonstrate that the immigrant Australian can share the xenophobia of the Australian-born. One of the defining anti-conscription posters of the time said, simply: 'Vote No and keep Australia white'.

What makes Australia unique, even as it struggles to shape a new identity for itself in a borderless world, is that we still absorb immigrants faster than any other nation. We have a persuasive example in our lifetime: Asian immigration, which moved from being the bogey of the 1980s to a non-issue today. Absorption into Australian society takes roughly one generation, the time an immigrant needs to work, start a family, and see his or her children into university. We are a better model than the United States, because we are closer to the middle-class ideal. Also, let's face it, successive governments have run an open, although selective immigration program. We don't practise the laissez-faire policy of the US, which doesn't mind using unskilled foreigners to bid down local wage-rates. The distance between rich and poor in Australia is not as great as in the US, which is why our women and immigrants, with a little education, have been able to surpass 'white' men over the past 20 years. Yet income is the reason Sydney is the most hostile host to immigration. It is the most US-style city we have, where the economics of intolerance loom largest. But even Sydney can be persuaded.

In August 1988, John Howard, then opposition leader, said we were importing too many Asians:

> I wouldn't like it [the rate of Asian immigration] to be greater. I'm not in favour of going back to the White Australia policy. I do believe that, if it is in the eyes of some in the community it's too great, it would be in our immediate-term interest and supporting of social cohesion if it were slowed down a little, so the capacity of the community to absorb it was greater.

By this stage, the so-called 'Asian debate' was four years old, courtesy of the repeated warnings by historian Geoffrey Blainey. In 1984, Blainey posed a dilemma he thought he already knew the answer to. If Australia didn't wake up to its folly it would become 'Asianised'. He said:

> It is public opinion which ultimately decides whether an immigration program will succeed. At present, the [Hawke] Government is shunning a vital section of public opinion. It is in the interests of those who are already here, and especially those who have contributed so much to this country, that the pace of Asian immigration should be slower.[13]

Fast forward to 1996, and Pauline Hanson's maiden speech to federal parliament:

> I believe we are in danger of being swamped by Asians. Between 1984 and 1995, 40 per cent of all immigrants coming into this country were of Asian origin. They have their own culture and religion, form ghettos and do not assimilate.[14]

Clearly, if you juxtapose Blainey's complaint with Hanson's cry, Australia was losing the race. But the historian from Melbourne and the MP from Ipswich, south of Brisbane, both got it wrong.

Guess which conservative politician would eventually confirm the errors of Blainey and Hanson? Sydney-centric Howard. Asian immigration, unlike reconciliation, is an issue on which Howard has been prepared to utter the s-word: sorry. The process of contrition began in January 1995, when Howard prepared to claim the opposition leadership from Alexander Downer. Howard felt he needed to clear the air on his earlier anti-Asian immigration comments:

> I'm sorry that my remarks were seen by people, Australians, if they were seen by Australians of Asian descent as suggesting that I regarded them in any way as lesser Australians than any other Australians then I regret that very much. That was never my intention. In the nature of politics, I don't know how a bloke can be more explicit.[15]

In an interview with me in April 2002, the Prime Minister made a series of concessions that added to that apology. First, he revealed that his stance in 1988 was a factor in losing the opposition leadership:

> I got chucked out of the leadership not long after that [May 1989]. I don't know how far that set me back. Those words weren't all that well-phrased at the time, but it's not something that anybody, and I don't mean it rudely, anybody except historical journalists thought about.

Howard also volunteered that Asian–Australians had done better than many thought possible: 'my instinct is that Asian–Australians are very much part of the community now'. Eager to run a line of my own by him, I asked if he saw Chinese–Australians and Vietnamese–Australians as the new Greeks and Italians? 'Yeah I do, very much so, yes. I think it has been quicker.' This begged the follow-up question: had the debate been settled against Blainey? 'To some extent it has, yes I agree with that.' Finally, Howard said that the Australia which Blainey was talking about had grown up, and shed 'the sharper edge of multiculturalism':

> What older Australians felt threatened about with some aspects of multiculturalism was the feeling that it required them to, in some ways, distance themselves from what they identified with — to repudiate traditional Australia. I think that's gone. People are in a way more interested in our traditional history ... in our war history and the Federation and all of that now than you had even ten years ago.[16]

I expected, at this point, that he would claim full credit for this process. But he admitted that his views had also changed along the way. Howard spoke during the 2001 election about the Asian–Australian faces at his son Tim's 21st birthday party, held a couple of years earlier. It would have been an intriguing moment for onlookers; the son introducing to his father the friends whose parents may not have made the trip to Australia had Howard prevailed a decade earlier. The redeeming part of this story is that politicians are not as powerful as they think. Howard, and then Hanson, thought there were votes to be won by targeting Asians. But they misjudged how quickly Asian–Australians became members of Generation W.

The notion that politicians can play a race card against Australian voters, be they 'yellow'- or 'olive'-skinned, has become as passé as the video-cassette recorder, although some still use these methods. The past two decades of economic reform has helped accelerate the integration of immigrants. Don't take my word for it; it was Howard who said that Orientals have been accepted faster than the first wave of southern Europeans. Of course, we needed a new victim, the asylum-seeker, to prove this. But the war on boat people in 2001 wasn't a race election in the traditional sense of the term, because it didn't pit voter against voter — with the possible exception of western Sydney — although, even there, the urban myth may not be all that it seems. Please suspend your judgement on this front until you read about the secret polling conducted by the main parties that is revealed in the second half of this book.

⁂ ⁂ ⁂

When Howard was elected to power in 1996, he took an axe to the immigration program, and old Australia applauded. It took him three years to realise that he was wrong, that the Australian economy needed more, not less, workers from overseas if it were to continue growing at the pace that voters in both the city and bush demanded. In 2002, Howard returned the immigration intake to above 100,000 — a figure Paul Keating never touched when he was prime minister between 1991 and 1996. Howard could lift immigration numbers without being seen as a hypocrite because people did not believe him to be pro-immigration. Yet that is what he became. Howard was careful to stack these larger intakes with skilled immigrants, to correct the excess of Bob Hawke's emphasis on family reunion in the 1980s.

It is a formula that the electorate approves of. The danger, though, in insisting that new arrivals are wealthy and over-qualified, is that their children blow their inheritance and fail to match the results of Generation W. The other risk is that skilled immigrants become mercenaries, willing to hop between first-world nations that offer them the fattest pay packet. As the *Economist* noted in 2002:

> Poor countries are not the only ones affected by outward migration. Australia and Canada not only lose their own people to the United States. They also find, to their irritation, that the most skilled immigrants use them as entrepot countries, acquiring citizenship and education before moving on to the largest and richest job market in the world.[17]

The brain drain, the serial whinge that Australia keeps losing its brightest overseas may, in fact, be accentuated by skilled immigration. This is another way of appreciating Generation W, the offspring of unskilled immigrants. Their loyalty to Australia, as well as their value to the economy, has been proven.

We now need a new word to understand what Generation W, the women and immigrants, are doing together to the nation. Let's employ 'snagging'. In its most basic form, snagging is the compromise we strike when we prowl around for a partner. It begins with the word games involved in the first encounter with someone we are interested in. For men, the bluff involves books. The true male snagger will wait until she volunteers her favourite authors; that way, he only needs two bits of fiction to keep the conversation going. He gushes over one of the titles she has mentioned, and then takes a guess at one she hasn't. 'What a coincidence, I bought *Almost French* the other day. It's next on my list, after I've finished *Ulysses*.' The gamble here is that she hasn't read either Homer or James Joyce. If she has, he probably won't be that keen after all. For girls, the ruse is football or rugby. If a woman snagger meets someone who says he has something other than CDs on his bookshelf, she will feign an open mind about going to a game. The goal for both sides is to appear interesting enough to snag a date.

Snagging is what politicians do for a living. The good ones convince us that they are important to our lives. We call them leaders. We can recite many of the views of Howard, Keating, or Hanson because they make us listen. Their distinctive voices are as unique, though not necessarily as loveable, as those of celebrities. They don't have to be correct, just persuasive enough to jolt the way we think as a nation.

The secret to successful snagging is that you can't make the play without changing along the way. The guy knows he will end up buying a copy of *Love in the Time of Cholera*; otherwise he won't survive the grilling at their big dinner. If the girl insists on keeping her end of the bargain and attends a match, she may be hooked. Likewise, politicians are forced to adapt. The successful ones inevitably bend at the altar of the ballot box, so they are, in a sense, the ultimate snaggers. Men and women may revert after the initial blush of romance wears off. Politicians, on the other hand, always try to second-guess society. Howard's Asian epiphany is snagging at its best.

Democracy in the age of policy sameness has been reduced to

a contest between poll-driven pick-up lines. The banter that works best is what we want to hear, so they often follow us, not the other way around. The numbers at federal elections are still with old Australia, as 2001 demonstrated. But the anti-war demonstrations of 2003 suggest that new Australia is ready to be mobilised. Generation W is closer to where Australia is heading than those who decided the last election.

Between them, successful women and immigrants are softening the nation, making it both less ocker and more cosmopolitan. The chap who proves this is the twenty- and thirty-something 'white' male. They call him the 'metrosexual', and swimmer Ian Thorpe is held up as Australia's exhibit A. Thorpey is a post-macho male, a sporting hero who wears Armani. He is, in effect, a wannabe wog boy, an Australian mimicking the well-dressed continental men who started appearing on shore after World War II. A guy who takes care in his appearance is paying tribute to both parts of Generation W, the women and the children of immigrants. He knows he won't impress anyone if Paul Hogan's character is his benchmark for manhood, beer stubby in hand, Winnie Blue in the other, a pair of stubbies and a Chesty Bond as his uniform.

Looking back, it appears that Keating, the champion of new Australia, was an early model metrosexual with his Zegna suits and cheer squad of higher-income women. Only his language let him down — one aspect was direct from the backstreets of old Australia, the other from the too-smart-by-halves new Australia. No wonder both old and new Australia voted him out equally in the end.

THESE PHOTOS PROVE THERE ARE WOMEN ON BOARDS AND THEY'RE NOT BEING THROWN OFF....
CHAIRMAN
2001: THE TAMPON CRISIS..

CHAPTER TWO

Women and Work

'Many parents desire, for at least the early years in a child's life, for one of the parents to be providing full-time child care.'
—John Howard, election campaign launch, 1996

OKAY, TRICK QUESTION. How long did the vanguard of women's liberation, the Helen Reddy 'hear me roar' generation of the 1970s, stay out of the workforce after having children? Two, perhaps three, years? Or when the kids were ready for kindergarten? Sorry, but we'd be remembering an era that never was. Numbers too big to ignore from the 1976 census show that women waited until their youngest child was packed off to primary school. A typical mother with two children spent up to a decade at home. Only when the youngest child was aged six to 13 years did a majority of mothers have jobs. Even then, barely half the women in this group were employed: 51 per cent. The radicalism of the second wave of feminism was a mirage. Germaine Greer's sisters behaved no differently, on average, than the mothers of Robert Menzies's whitegoods-loving 1950s. In 1976, the configuration of husband as breadwinner and wife as full-time mother was as mainstream as watching 'The Sullivans' on television.

Nothing much had changed a decade later when the first daughters of the women's movement had themselves reached motherhood. In 1986, women still sported aprons. The threshold between work and home remained the same: women took jobs when their youngest child was aged between six and 13 years.[1] This is the first warning that something is amiss in Australia today. The generation that runs government and business — baby boomer-and-older men — did their procreating in another epoch, when women tended to be full-time mothers for the best part of their twenties. This wouldn't be a problem if twenty- and thirty-somethings today had followed the same path to early marriage and extended maternity. But they didn't. Not only did these women wait longer to have babies, they had fewer of them, and they went back to work sooner than any group before them.

The women of new Australia are from Venus, and their baby-boomer predecessors are from Pluto. Here's why. By 1996, the typical mother returned to work after her youngest child turned three years of age. Fifty-four per cent had jobs and, compared to the stasis of the previous four decades, time off for raising children had halved. Then, in 2001, the majority moved again; women went back to work when their youngest child was one to two years old, and 51 per cent of mothers were employed. In the space of a decade, the Australian family had moved from a single-income to a two-income operation.

Social researchers tell us that most women would prefer to stay at home for a time after having a baby. But the 2001 census shows that the majority can't afford not to work. Mothers who chose to quickly resume employment during John Howard's first five years in office were either in low-income households or had high-paying careers. This reduced the single-income family to an enclave for a pampered middle — the couples where men were earning enough to allow women to stay at home if they wanted to — without sacrificing too much of their pre-baby lifestyle.

Blame this shift on uber-materialism. We are trained to expect exponential growth. A once-in-a-century technological boom has seen the gadgets that baby boomers viewed as luxury items in their childhood — televisions, hi-fis, and cars — become disposable commodities in the new millennium. The mantra of consumerism is to trade up, from the VCR to the DVD, from the family pool table to the PlayStation, from the stereo TV to the plasma screen. Mobile phone companies make their profits from making us think a phone generation runs for about a year, which is why they want us to update our handsets like children do with their toys and computer games.

We've got more rooms in our houses, on average, and fewer people in them. Living in the 1970s meant that the typical household didn't have bedrooms for each member. In 1971, the average household had 3.3 people in it, and the most common house had two bedrooms (36 per cent of the total). By 2001, the average household had shrunk to 2.6 people, yet the proportion of two-bedroom houses had been reduced to 27 per cent, while the four-bedroom house had almost doubled its share from 13 per cent to 25 per cent over the same time-frame.[2] We need two incomes to live this way, so when we add the expense of another life to the calculation, why do politicians still scratch their heads when women take the first opportunity to work again? The longer a mother stays out of the workplace, the bigger the risk that the job she goes back to will be beneath her, or gone.

There are also home loan repayments to consider. In 2003, a worker on average earnings of $49,000 a year does not qualify for a mortgage for a typical home in each of the mainland capital cities. A second income is required to impress the bank manager. In Sydney, a couple needs 2.3 times average earnings to afford a $431,100 property. In Melbourne, a couple earning 1.7 times above the average qualifies for a $311,200 house. In Canberra, a couple needs 1.6 times average earnings for a

$299,700 property; in Brisbane 1.4 and $254,500 respectively; and in Perth and Adelaide, an income 1.1 times the average could buy houses worth $211,600 and $206,200 respectively.[3]

So we'd expect that politicians would wonder what happens to the typical Australian child in the years before the state assumes the role of primary carer through the school system? Er, no. In the lead-up to the 2001 federal election, child care rated as a lower priority for debate between John Howard's coalition government and Kim Beazley's Labor opposition than whether the Goods and Services Tax (GST) should apply to tampons. We can't blame them. The strategic geniuses who came up with this hierarchy of women's needs were baby-boomer-and-older men. It didn't seem to occur to them that the new women were different to their own wives. One feisty adviser to the then opposition leader says there was also a snigger factor at play: 'Our blokes just wanted to say the word "tampon"'.

The communication breakdown between women and the men who run government and business starts here, with the topic men know the least about: motherhood. In a 50 per cent-plus-one democracy such as ours, the majority of female professional workers and working mothers with toddlers should buy some respect. They haven't, so far. The better-qualified woman of new Australia still earns less than men of her age. The rip-off starts at the top of the tree with the legal profession. Twenty- and thirty-something women lawyers outnumber their male counterparts 53 per cent to 47 per cent. Yet if we check the pay of those in Generation W aged 25–34 years, there is a 12 per cent gap in the men's favour. The median income for women is $1201 a week; for men, $1342. The deficit is greater still for those working 36 hours or more a week.

The explanation is babies, right? No. These are the figures for women lawyers aged 25–34 years without children. It is the same catch for their childless peers in other occupations in the new economy. Women computer professionals are 14 per cent behind their male colleagues. Visit a Generation W general practitioner, and she will pocket 11 per cent less than the typical male doctor. Even in nursing, where women hold three out of every four jobs, the younger, career-driven ones are still 10 per cent shy of male nurses at the same age.[4] The income deficit for educated women is compounded by their inability to claim the positions of manager and administrator. In August 2001, women held just 28 per cent of the 765,000 positions of authority in the economy, a snail's paced improvement on the 25 per cent of a decade earlier. Women may have broken through in the professional workforce, but the glass ceiling is still to be cracked.[5]

The weight of government policies remains tilted towards the baby-boomer mother who stays at home for five or more years to raise her children. This tension became apparent when Howard unveiled his domestic agenda at the climax of the 2001 election. The campaign launch is a set piece where the candidate gets to talk directly into the living rooms of ordinary Australians without the distraction of an opponent or interviewer. It is generally accepted that this televised address will yield a boost in the polling of the party concerned. At his campaign launch, Howard sought to impress the professional woman. He offered her a payment of between $500 and $2500 a year to encourage her to have children, which he dubbed the 'baby bonus'. The handout was based on women's pre-maternity income, with the maximum amount going to those who were earning more than $55,000 a year.

The policy recognised that women wanted a career before motherhood. However, the gesture went down badly with the electorate. The blip was immaterial to the final election result. Nevertheless, what Howard saw in microcosm was the difficulty politicians would have in communicating with a double-income society. The unpopularity of the baby bonus stemmed from its unreality. To collect the full amount of $12,500, the mother would have to stay at home for five years. After the election, Howard said his government would consider paid maternity leave as an option to help families.

* * *

The clumsily termed 'work–family' debate that began in earnest in 2002 shows that Generation W has the ability to rattle the cage of government. Howard's first five years in office saw fewer people marrying, and fewer women having children than during the previous five years of Paul Keating's Labor government. Which goes to show that people don't pay that much attention to their leaders. Otherwise, the period 1996–2001 would have seen more women reporting for duty in the maternity wards and in the kitchen instead of the office.

A trio of Australia's big social trends intersect with twenty- and thirty-something women: the transformation of the economy; the baby bust; and the relative dumbing-down of men. Discussion about what should happen next is bogged on a counter-intuitive track. Both sides of politics still think they can clone their ideal family. The right wants supermum to once again be free to run the household; the left wants supermum to run the household and also reign in the boardroom. In chasing these stereotypes, politicians and activists forget the real world where most women are on time-and-a-half — full-time mum and permanent part-time worker.

Freedom of choice, which both right and left claim as a common value, is best facilitated by letting people work it out for themselves. This means a policy for each choice, not a policy wand to wave away those who don't fit one's preconception of Australia. The goal should be to remove the guilt, so women feel less pressured to work or stay at home. This is not a task for governments alone, but for the boss and the partner, because politicians in particular are always the last to figure out what women want. Our economy demands a more elastic worker than ever before. If the majority of professionals are women, male employers should apply business nous. They are better off giving their staff paid maternity leave and malleable hours rather than risk losing them to a competitor who will.

* * *

Howard has openly carried the image of father at work and mother at home as his political talisman. It was on the cover of his 1988 manifesto, 'Future Directions'. That document was considered out-of-date then, and was one of the lesser reasons why he failed to keep his job as opposition leader in 1989. But those who followed — Andrew Peacock, John Hewson, and Alexander Downer — had even less luck with the electorate, which kept returning Labor governments. This cycle of defeat convinced the Liberals to give Howard his old job back in a bloodless coup in 1995. On his return to power, Howard recognised that the single-income family was a minority trend. Even so, he had a powerful incentive to rebuild his icon. Mothers at home still mattered at the ballot box in the 1990s, a point that Howard's feminist critics seem to ignore. These conservative women were the voters who cost the coalition the 1993 GST election because they didn't like Hewson's plan to gut Medicare. Howard saw that he had to court this group in 1996 if he wanted any chance of becoming prime minister. He needed these women again in 1998, when he revived the GST that he had said would 'never ever' be coalition policy again.

The full-time mother received the most generous tax cuts in Howard's first two terms as prime minister, and became the main beneficiary of the only personal tax cut he could afford at the 2001 election, the baby bonus. The combined booty was worth almost $3 billion a year, although the baby bonus accounted for less than 10 per cent of the total. At the end of 1999, when he was aged 60, Howard explained the slant of his family policies:

> I have probably done more as prime minister in changing the tax laws to help single-income [families] than any prime minister in the [past] 30 years.[6]

Translation: he saw himself as the greatest defender of the father-at-work, mother-at-home ideal since Menzies.

Yet Howard's family tax cuts were too small to change the way people conducted their lives. There was a mass movement under way which could not be tempered with a payment of a few thousand dollars a year. The typical mother trimmed another one or two years between kitchen and career on his watch. In August 2001, the majority of mothers with a youngest child aged one to two years worked. Almost half of this group were in jobs that took 25 hours or more a week of their time. Those who chose to remain at home with a toddler had shrunk from 48 per cent in 1996 to 46 per cent in 2001. The only segment in which most mothers were still at home was when they had a baby aged less than twelve months. Yet even here, 35 per cent now had jobs. In 1976, the employment rate in this group was a mere 15 per cent.

Howard defines his battlers as those families on $20,000–$50,000 a year. These former Labor supporters from whom he has drawn his electoral strength are the key to understanding the duality of the nation today. The battlers comprise the section of society with a foot in both camps, old and new Australia. It is the battlers who are the crucial defector that turns the working mother into an increasing majority, despite

Howard's best efforts to allow her to stay at home. In 1996, lower-income couples on $400–$799 a week ($20,800–$41,458 a year) represented 49 per cent of all single-income families with young children. This is proof that Howard was pitching to real people when he became prime minister. But the battlers went back to work. In 2001, they dropped to 29 per cent. Taking their place as the pin-up for the single-income family were the well-off families on $1000–$1999 a week ($52,000–$103,948 a year), who rose from 15 per cent to 38 per cent of the total.[7]

The battlers are no longer over-represented in the ranks of father-at-work, mother-at-home families compared with the national income-distribution for all families. Mothers in households that earn more than $2000 a week ($104,000 a year) have also resumed their careers in even larger proportions. Both groups are more likely than not to be Liberal voters in the federal parliament, and supporters of Labor's 'BBC' at the state level — Bracks, Beattie, and Carr, the premiers who cover the eastern seaboard of Victoria, Queensland, and New South Wales. That's why they persuaded Howard to talk up the idea of paid maternity leave after the 2001 election. The baby bonus was going to mothers in the middle class, the politically correct Labor voter in inner-city Sydney and Melbourne. These families, on household incomes of $1000–$1999 a week, moved from being under- to over-representative of single-income families with young children between 1996 and 2001.

I asked the Australian Bureau of Statistics to dig out this data from its unpublished census material going back to the mid-1970s. I published the first of the findings, coincidently, on the day I bumped into the Prime Minister at a social function, as one does in journalism in Canberra.[8] One of the things that separates politicians from the rest of the community — apart from their can't-lose superannuation plan — is that they never stop talking about work, even on nights off. Howard had absorbed the

Saturday papers that morning, so I couldn't escape a chat without his verdict on my article, 'New Woman No Cry'. Once we had dispensed with small talk, Howard volunteered that he had read what I had written. In good spirits, he said it was 'very interesting'. But there was a paragraph he didn't agree with, where I'd predicted, cheekily, that in a decade from now most women would be asking the boss for time off to blow out the candle on their baby's first birthday cake. The proportion of new mothers who were at home in the first twelve months after childbirth had fallen steadily from 83 per cent in 1976, to 71 per cent in 1986, to 65 per cent in 1996, and to 63 per cent in 2001. Howard corrected me, and said that this was not yet a tidal wave. It may well be the case that the majority of mothers will still take the first twelve months off work in 2011. This is something women should be free to choose.

⁂ ⁂ ⁂

There is a new woman to deal with in politics, one that is more likely to be insulted rather than placated by another version of the tax handouts that underwrote family life in old Australia. Howard was forced to consider policies that rubbed against his world view, and at a time when he was enjoying his highest approval rating as prime minister. This is a victory of sorts for Generation W. However, the sight of a leader being dragged, reluctantly, into the twenty-first century is also distressing. Democracy, as practised in Australia, cannot be said to be truly responsive if it takes a conservative government this long to figure out that the majority of new mothers have already been working for the best part of a decade.

It should not be hard for politicians to step into the shoes of women today. Working women are more 'male', in the career-absorbed sense of word, than any women before them. The median age of motherhood increased from 27 years in 1981 to 30 years in 2001.[9] Do the maths. That extra three years is corporate ladder-climbing. For Generation W women, their twenties have become the decade of advancement in contrast to the decade of nappies that was the baby-boomer woman's reality. The simple explanation is that women today have jobs worth keeping. It's the difference between the woman with a bachelor of law degree and the woman who learned to cook and sew after leaving high school; the allure of Generation W's life on Venus versus the baby boomer's more limited options on Pluto. This is not to imply that one generation is more content than the other, but to understand what drives them.

As any stressed twenty- or thirty-something woman will tell you, a career can't buy love, happiness, a mortgage-free mansion, or the time to read books. The creative power of capitalism is its ability to make us want what we can't have; otherwise we would stop going to work. Men have known this for more than a century and are miffed now that woman have joined the club. The rebirth of the Australian economy, from blue collar to what is now termed 'pink collar', can be seen in the two largest groups in the workforce. At the end of the recession in 1991, professionals numbered 1 million, or 15 per cent of all workers. Lawyers, doctors, and accountants were only just ahead of mechanics and bricklayers. Tradespeople were second on the ladder, with 980,000, or 14 per cent of all positions. Both rungs belonged to men: a fraction over 50 per cent of professionals were men, and 89 per cent of tradespeople. In short, a suit-and-singlet society.

That would prove to be the apotheosis of old Australia. In August 2001, the professional class had grown to 1.5 million, or 18 per cent of the workforce, and women had moved into the majority. Tradespeople, meanwhile, had slipped to third spot; their 1 million workers overtaken by 1.4 million sales and clerical staff, of which 72 per cent were women. So the top two places were in the hands of under-paid and low-paid women. Women should bear in mind that the architects of their economic power did not mean for them to take the free market so literally.

The two politicians who shaped our entry into the global marketplace are pre-baby-boomer men — Keating, born in 1944, and Howard, born in 1939. Sworn enemies, their animosity reflects the faultline between cosmopolitan and conservative Australia. Keating was the spear-carrier for the former; Howard is the defender of the latter. But beneath this personality and policy clash are two men with remarkably similar views on motherhood. Keating agreed with Howard that women shouldn't mix work with child-raising. Keating's former speech writer, Don Watson, confirmed in *Recollections of a Bleeding Heart* that Keating would sometimes mutter privately that 'the solution to unemployment was persuading women to leave the workforce':

> Of course, he could not go about the country urging women to go home, but he did continue to believe, albeit in ways modified by experience, that the home was the ideal place for women with children.[10]

This quote should assure us that one of the problems with politicians today is not the colour of their party membership card, but their gender.

In the 1980s, our politicians proved to be good at starting things. It was a decade that saw the most change dictated by a government outside of a world war. It was one of the few times that they snagged us. But once they exposed the economy to the cyclone of international competition, they ceded any control over the people who worked in it. It is a contradiction that Keating and, later, Howard, didn't seem to grasp: without the cocoon of tariffs, centralised wage-fixing, nine-to-five weekday hours, and the six o'clock close at the pub, it made less sense for governments to tell people when they should make babies and who should change the nappies. Howard is an economic liberal and social conservative, a free marketeer, and an occasional social engineer. The times may have suited him politically at the start of the new millennium, but the hard numbers of working families didn't vindicate his social agenda.

Work–family is one of those hopelessly bureaucratic terms that fail to define what we are supposed to be talking about. In new Australia, as in old Australia, we engage in discussion by buzz words. It is the dialogue of the deaf, in which opposing sides shout at one another from the trenches of their prejudice. But the argument that began in earnest after the refugee election of 2001 does carry a redeeming twist. It offers an unwitting concession from politicians that women may well be the equal of, if not superior to, men. In our recent high-protection past, when the economy was primarily male-only, the balance between work and family was not considered an issue. Men worked, and women took care of the children. Today, when voters complain about the pressure of juggling work and family, the subtext is that women are expected to do both. The real issue here is the failure of men to consider sharing the load. We would need the Hubble telescope to find the reverse single-income family of Mum at work and Dad at home. Barely one in every 100 has a mother working full-time and a father working as a full-time carer. Even the compromise of the woman working full-time and the man holding down a part-time job is a pipe dream — accounting for 2 per cent of families and 1 per cent of those with children aged 0–5 years.[11]

⁂ ⁂ ⁂

Education, the single largest cost involved in raising a child, is moving inexorably towards user-pays because the state systems have been allowed to regress. This is another contradiction that politicians at all levels who preach family values do not seem to understand. The proportion of families sending their children to private schools has been increasing steadily, from 30 per cent of secondary students in 1986 to 37 per cent in 2001.[12] The end of free university education in 1989 taught the present generation of graduates that spending, not saving, is a virtue. Those working today with a Higher Education Contributions Scheme (HECS) debt to the government are earning more, but are less likely to be homeowners than the baby boomers before them.

Generation HECS, graduates aged 25–34 years in 1998, earned $71,200 on average per household, but only 39 per cent were homeowners, either with a mortgage or freehold title. A decade earlier, in 1986, the last of the free university graduates earned $62,487 in today's dollars; yet more than half (54 per cent) already had their own home. Many of the well-paid members of Generation W are heading to middle age without the great Australian leg-up to prosperity: property.[13] In Sydney, the nation's most crowded and expensive capital city, and in Brisbane, the nation's youngest, there are now more people who have never owned a home than those who have mortgages.[14]

The women of new Australia, and their men, face the mother of all societal squeezes. The first giant leap in dismantling the walled economy of father at work and mother at home was taken in 1983 when the Labor government of Bob Hawke, with Keating as treasurer, floated the dollar. Keating then assumed effective leadership of the reform process while Howard, as opposition leader, gave him bipartisanship. Timing is everything. If Gough Whitlam hadn't opened up the university system to women a decade earlier, Australia would not have had the extra trained brain power to service the Keating–Howard economy. The immigration intake that would have been needed to fill the gap could not have survived the race debates of the 1980s and 1990s.

Having a paid job altered the dynamics of the mating game. The women of new Australia are a unique breed, the first to outsmart the men of their generation. The sexual dynamic of the 1970s was promiscuity, courtesy of the contraceptive pill. Today, we are a society that spends more time agonising to each other about the shortage of compatible partners than doing anything about it. It's the era of multiple choices without real options, because we can't have it all; and human nature being what it is, we never could. As academics keep telling us, men tend to be competitive beasts who prefer to marry down. This is another reason Australians are having fewer babies. Women have more reason to be choosy, which makes men all the more wary. This is the gridlock of Generation W.

Yet who is running the work–family debate for women? Who is countering the male politicians of the Keating–Howard generation? Baby-boomer feminists who, like their opponents, formed their opinions in another world. Howard, to his credit, was awake to the new woman before the Labor opposition was, and before many of his own cabinet ministers. His daughter, Melanie Howard, a twenty-something Sydney lawyer, may have had something to do with it. But the opinion polls, the hidden reef that ultimately grounds the out-of-touch politician, were the clincher. Howard's baby bonus fizzed at the 2001 election because the voters he cares about, the battlers, did not take it seriously. They were already back at work. It was political necessity that forced Howard to pare back his definition of the single-income family to the first twelve months of a child's life, instead of the 'early years' that he talked about at his 1996 election campaign launch.

Here's another scoop from the census. There *is* a family type that remains intact like families were in the 1970s, where women were found at home until their youngest child reached six to 13 years of age. Only there is no father. The stream of statistics quoted earlier is for two-parent households. Lone parents face a poverty trap that experts have ignored. Single mothers can't afford to go back to work, even if they wanted to. Try this number and see if it fits in with our idea of a multiple-choice society: 62 per cent of single parents are at home when their youngest child is aged one to two years. The unemployment rate for this group is above 9 per cent, more than three times the mothers in two-parent households.

So far, Australia's work–family debate has been concerned with how to preserve a middle-class lifestyle, not how to help the underclass. Middle-aged men and women, politicians, and activists pontificate from a comfort zone that misses the mainstream and the outcast. But there is ground for optimism. The sexual politics of the next generation should not be as warped as it is today. The women of new Australia are on edge because they have no role models to show them how to deal with men as qualified equals. The boys haven't done worse than their fathers; it is the girls who have eclipsed their mothers. Generation W is the wobbly bridge between old and new Australia.

A small sign that women are softening the nation can be found in the bedroom, where women are beginning to dump middle-aged men. The thirty-something woman today is more likely than her baby-boomer sister to be living with a younger man. Some 5 per cent of women in their thirties are in relationships with men in their twenties. In 1981, the figure was 3 per cent. Sure, this isn't the greatest surge in history. However, it means that the forty-something man is more likely to be with a woman in his own age-group than ever before, not counting any affairs either party might be conducting on the side. In August 2001, 64 per cent of men in their forties were with women in their forties, a marked difference on the 58 per cent in 1981.

Forty-something men who boast younger women as partners are moving onto the endangered-species list. The proportion of men in their forties who are partnered with women in their thirties dropped from 36 to 29 per cent over the same period. Middle-aged men with women in their twenties were virtual dodos — stuck at less than 2 per cent. On the other hand, women in their forties don't get to play with younger men to the same extent — they are represented on the census as an asterisk at less than 1 per cent. Perhaps that's a structural reform for Generation Z to consider.[15]

One lesson to be drawn here is that we shouldn't pay too much attention to Hollywood. The notion that a box office smash is supposed to reflect the times is a myth of marketing. The movie *The Graduate*, in which an older woman beds a younger man, would make more sense today than it did in the 1960s. Perversely, the TV series 'Sex in the City' is a generation out-of-date, where Carrie Bradshaw, the well-preened predator and narrator, invariably ends up in the sack with older men such as Mr Big. It is Samantha Jones who is closer to the present; but, as a forty-something, she is not always for real. Then again, what these two pieces of popular culture have in common is the middle-class dream: the young buck broken in by a more experienced woman (Mrs Robinson or Samantha), and the young woman too bright to sleep with men her own age (Carrie).

The challenge now is to find an advocate for Generation W from within its own ranks. This job is beyond the baby boomers. Male politicians do not have enough practical experience of life in new Australia to speak with authority; neither do old left feminists, nor the right, who stay at home and snarl from their laptops. The nation can only start playing the issue when the debate is in the hands of those who know the differences between the old and new woman. The hitch is, as history shows, that this generation may take power too late, and rule after society has managed to strike some sort of truce in the gender wars. A government run by women may be just as misguided in its dealings with the next generation as the Keating–Howard men are now. But that's the physics of politics: for every over-reaction there has to be an equally absurd over-correction.

DOES IT RAIN MUCH IN MELBOURNE?..
HARDLY A DAGO'S DAY GOES BY...

CHAPTER THREE

Sydney vs Melbourne

'Sydney has always been much more racist than Melbourne.'
—Liberal Party powerbroker, November 2001

IT IS EASY TO FORGET how 'white' the working-class heart of Sydney was only a generation ago. In 1981, Bankstown, in the city's industrial west, the birthplace of cricketing twins Steve and Mark Waugh, boasted a lower immigrant intake than Mosman, the nation's wealthiest suburb on the unobtainable north shore. The Australian-born population in Bankstown was 75 per cent; in Mosman, it was 73 per cent. To appreciate how unusual this rate of peroxide was for a working-class suburb at that time, look back towards the city, to Marrickville, in Sydney's inner west. In 1981, Marrickville was on the cusp of becoming a fifty–fifty postcode with a local-born contingent of just 53 per cent and falling.[1]

Bankstown had also been home to Paul Keating, whose formative years in the 1940s and 1950s were scarred by sectarianism — Australia's third significant burst of race angst after it dispossessed Australian Aboriginals on settlement, and the Chinese on the goldfields a century later. The ethnic gangs that Australia worried about in those days were Irish-Catholic. Keating took to using the word 'tyke' in the way that Greek– and Italian–Australians would later use 'wog', as an in-joke to assert his inclusion in a society that had previously been wary towards his caste. Don't, however, confuse Keating's outcast upbringing for a cosmopolitan inheritance. The bleaching of Bankstown meant that Keating would have known relatively fewer immigrants than John Howard did while growing up in Earlwood, which neighbours Marrickville.

When Sydney opened its door to non-English-speaking immigrants after World War II, the new arrivals favoured the cheap damp terraces and workers' cottages of the inner suburbs. Like Nino Culotta in *They're A Weird Mob*, they all wanted the directions to Kings a-bloody Cross. The middle-ring suburbs such as Bankstown were unaffected by immigration. This is one of the main reasons Sydney is different to Melbourne on race. Bankstown's battler-identikit by shape and distance from the CBD is Sunshine in Melbourne's middle west. Unlike Bankstown, Sunshine was in the immigration game from the moment the first continentals berthed at Port Melbourne after World War II. In 1981, quarter-acre Sunshine had more in common with crowded Marrickville than it did with Bankstown, with just 59 per cent of its residents being Australian-born. By August 2001, the overseas-born were an entrenched majority, leaving the local-born at 46 per cent of the suburb. Yet the Melbourne media did not shriek 'white flight' or 'Asian ghettoes' at the release of these statistics, because more immigrants in Sunshine was neither news nor was it seen as a problem. Unlike Sydney, Melbourne shared the immigration load across its working-class suburbs, inner and middle, from the outset.

When I began journalism in 1986, on a graduate cadetship with Melbourne's *Sun News Pictorial*, I was given some interesting career advice. My six-letter Christian name and eleven-letter surname were too long for the tabloid's format, which deemed that a reporter's by-line should run over a single slither between headline and news copy. One of the senior news editors suggested I chop off a few letters to conform. I was somewhere between the second and third phases of wogdom at the time, so I flashed him an idiot grin to deflect his request. He must have been satisfied that his jibe was harmless, because he didn't repeat it. And my name remained intact.

A few months later, I fielded a call from an ethnic group protesting its treatment at the hands of another, more 'popular' community. Let's say, for argument's sake, that it was a Martian organisation complaining about the better-connected people from Jupiter. I took the message to the chief of staff, who said we would not cover the rally to be held that day because it would trigger a letter-writing campaign from both sides. This would not be a good look for our conservative readership. My boss told me that the newspaper preferred to avoid stories that divided people in this way, so the event was quietly ignored.

The old *Sun News Pictorial*, as its banner suggested, was big on pictures. It saw the *Women's Weekly* as its main competitor for the latest gossip on Kylie Minogue when she was still Charlene in 'Neighbours'. Its sister tabloid in Sydney, the *Daily Telegraph,* which I also wrote for from the News Limited Canberra bureau, felt the same way about the soaps. But not race. In Sydney, a tiff between ethnic lobbies would have been a yarn worth running. At a raw commercial level, the contrasting reactions were a symptom of the two distinctive markets. Immigrants were more likely than not to be *Sun* subscribers; and they read the tabloid; like everyone else, from back to front. Common business sense dictated that they should not be confronted with an article that pitted one section of cosmopolitan Melbourne against another. The *Telegraph*, on the other hand, drew its readership strength from western Sydney, a more homogenous audience that was 'whiter' and less familiar with immigrants generally. It was also a louder, and decidedly politically incorrect, journal. The story would have been seen as harmless because it did not carry the risk of a reader backlash from those who might take it too seriously.

The Sydney media, both print and radio, serve a gridlocked city with a settlement pattern that is more warped than Melbourne's. Bankstown was a late bloomer to immigration. After missing out on the first batch of arrivals from Europe, it took the bulk of the second, from Asia and the Middle East. In 1981, the largest immigrant group in Bankstown was from the United Kingdom and Ireland — 6 per cent of the suburb's total population — followed by immigrants from Italy and Yugoslavia on 2 per cent each. In August 2001, Bankstown's Australian-born ranks had shrunk to 58 per cent, and the top three immigrants came from Lebanon and Vietnam (on 6 per cent each), and China (2 per cent). It is not hard to understand why they went to Bankstown. By the late 1980s, inner Sydney had become too pricey for both a struggling immigrant and a 'white' working-class home buyer.

Nevertheless, the immigrant concentrations in western Sydney today are mild by the standards of the old catchments of inner Sydney, and inner and western Melbourne. The Bankstown of 2001 was a mere 1 per cent more cosmopolitan than Sunshine had been 20 years earlier. In 1981, Bankstown was still a percentage point 'whiter' than the Sydney average. But two decades later, it had become 9 per cent more foreign. It is the pace of change that is at the heart of the problem, not the people that Sydney imports. Without the initial wave of Greeks and Italians to get used to, the second-wave Vietnamese and Lebanese gave Bankstown — the tabloid and talkback radio hearth of old Australia — a culture shock. Sydney was a cycle behind Melbourne, and this affected its whole attitude towards immigration.

* * *

In 2002, western Sydney was ranked as the least tolerant area in the nation — eclipsing even Pauline Hanson's Ipswich. In July 2002 the first university study of its type to try to measure 'racism' (their term, not mine) was released, titled 'Everywhere Different: A Geography of Racism'. The report, by Macquarie University and the University of New South Wales, focused on attitudes in New South Wales and Queensland. Academics decided that Victoria was not worth checking because residents were less troubled by new faces in the neighbourhood. The results proved to be provocative, despite their predictability. Canterbury–Bankstown recorded the strongest anti-Muslim sentiment. A majority of those questioned (53 per cent) said they would be concerned if a relative married a Muslim. This is the rawest indicator of prejudice, the *Guess Who's Coming to Dinner?* test. The most welcoming area studied was inner Sydney, where immigrants had been digested long ago. The most encouraging finding, though, was that Asian–Australians were now accepted by the wider community. The 'yellow' were found to be marginally more popular than the 'black'; 72 per cent of those surveyed said they would not mind an Asian in-law, compared to 71 per cent for an Australian Aboriginal in-law.[2]

Coincidently, in the same week that the report came out, two sets of brutal crimes echoed the contrast between Sydney and Melbourne. It was like living in a parallel universe. In Sydney, the courts handed down the first set of guilty verdicts to the gang rapists. It was the cue for the Sydney media to resume its race debate. The froth and fury of the city's talkback radio programs reaffirmed that many callers didn't like Muslims generally and interchanged the criminals with the Lebanese community they came from. Meanwhile, in Melbourne, three Vietnamese–Australian boys were murdered by members of a rival group of Vietnamese–Australians. But the Melbourne media reported on the attacks in the posh neighbourhood of

South Yarra with sensitivity. Police and press alike shied away from describing the murders as ethnic gang violence; and in many instances the background of the victims and their attackers was not even spelt out.

The question worth asking here is what the Sydney media would have done if both crimes had occurred within their jurisdiction. The gang rapes would still have been the bigger story, because they carried the extra edge of random menace; the idea that any woman in civilised society could have been a victim. But, in all likelihood, in Sydney the triple killings would have carried the taint of the ethnic gang for Vietnamese–Australians. In Sydney, the press routinely pushes the button marked 'sensational'. It would never self-censor itself in the same way that the Melbourne media does. On race, Sydney and Melbourne could well be from Mercury and Saturn: one white-hot, the other seemingly serene. The difference between the cities is cultural and economic. It starts with the altered settlement patterns and is reinforced by a contest as old as federation: free trade versus protection.

Sydney has traditionally been the first to question immigration. In the late 1940s, when the nation began importing non-English speakers en masse, historian Geoffrey Bolton said the resistance to these foreigners came from 'the RSL, the Australian Communist Party ... and sections of the Sydney media'. On the other hand, Melbourne tended to run ahead of national opinion and was eager to take on even more immigrants. In the early 1960s, the first lobby group to agitate for an end to the white Australia policy was spawned at the University of Melbourne, which is located in the little Italy of Carlton, one of Melbourne's many versions of Marrickville.[3]

The latest phase of Sydney's race angst has its roots in the tsunami of economic reforms unleashed by Keating in the 1980s, and consolidated by Howard in the second half of the 1990s.

The economy of Sydney, centre for the fast-money world of globalisation, kicked clear of Melbourne, bastion of the nation's sheltered manufacturing sector. Sydney sailed through recession in 1990–1, while Melbourne plunged into near-depression. The immigrants, naturally, went to where the economic action was. So Sydney replaced Melbourne as the city of choice for new arrivals. The catch is that the second wave of immigration went to suburbs that had not been softened by the first wave. This was also a time of much higher unemployment than Australians were accustomed to. The low-skilled workers who were once guaranteed work on arrival in Melbourne faced another world in Sydney, where jobs were being shed in the name of economic reform. Immigrants who went to Sydney were more likely to be seen as competitors by the local working class than they had been a generation earlier in Melbourne. As a child growing up in Melbourne, I was aware that my parents, and their friends, had taken jobs that old Australians would not. This would not be the case in Sydney.

However, someone forgot to tell Melbourne-centric Labor prime minister Bob Hawke that the ground rules for immigration were being overturned by the economy that his government was building. In the final three years of the 1980s, as we went boom then bust, Australia was importing more people — after subtracting those departing its shores — than it was replacing through babies. The problem was with the mix: the emphasis moved from low-skilled to family reunion, so many new immigrants were too old to be employed.[4] Hawke could not have picked a more fraught occasion to give the nation its three highest, and relatively least-productive, intakes in a generation. Sydney, the unwilling host, was getting most of the new arrivals and placing many of them directly onto welfare queues. Labor pulled back immigration when the Sydney-centric Keating became prime minister in 1991. The Bankstown boy reduced the number of people coming to Australia, and switched the emphasis to skilled immigrants. The similarly Sydney-centric Howard extended this policy after 1996. But this did not slow immigration to Sydney, which received almost twice as many immigrants as Melbourne. From 1 January 1991 to 31 December 2001, Sydney hosted 301,000 immigrants versus Melbourne's 177,000.[5]

Sydney was the nation's fourth-largest immigrant city in 1981, with 26 per cent of its citizens born overseas. Perth was first, at 32 per cent; Melbourne second, at 28 per cent; and Adelaide third, at 27 per cent. Two decades of economic upheaval later, and Sydney has top spot, with 33 per cent; Perth is a fraction behind; and Melbourne has slipped to third, at 30 per cent.[6] For Sydney, the city with the widest gap between rich and poor, this was a recipe for friction. The tension today between new and old Australia is upside down. Sydney is the nation's first global city, but its attitudes on race reflect the backlash of an old culture. Melbourne is closer to the new Australia of women and immigrants because it has had more time to adjust to the idea of Generation W.

The swing from Melbourne to Sydney has thrown up some quirks. The two cities remain equals because virtually every significant immigrant group has an anchor in each. Sydney and Melbourne have shared roughly fifty–fifty of the 'olive' and 'yellow' from Italy, Greece, China, and Vietnam. But there is one notable exception, which reveals another angle into why Sydneysiders see race through a harsher prism than Melburnians. By August 2001, 73 per cent of all Lebanese immigrants to Australia lived in Sydney. So the gang rapes, the *Tampa*, and September 11 — the trifecta that stoked Sydney's prejudice in the new millennium — came with a ready-made scapegoat.

It will pain supporters of immigration — especially the sophisticates in inner Sydney — but Howard was no historical accident. In the late 1980s, he embodied the duality of the Sydneysider. As an economic liberal, he niggled the Hawke–Keating government to go faster on policies such as privatisation and industrial relations. As a social conservative, he called for a pause on immigration. In 1988, he chose Sydney's then talkback radio king, John Laws, to launch his most infamous attack on Asian immigration. Perhaps Howard would not have worried if he had been bred as a politician from Melbourne, the home of his hero Robert Menzies. The prevailing ethos in Melbourne in the 1980s was for government intervention in the economy and political correctness. At the 1988 Victorian state election, held just after Howard criticised Asian immigration, the then Labor premier, John Cain, and his Liberal opponent, Jeff Kennett, struck a campaign pact not to mention race. This gentleman's agreement was explained to me by both politicians at the time, who said that Melbourne was a tolerant city, and that neither side wanted to be responsible for 'bricks being thrown through windows'. In the second half of the 1990s, Howard as Prime Minister was slow to rebuke Hanson's anti-immigration jihad. It was left to the Melbourne-born Treasurer, Peter Costello, to denounce her.

However, don't mistake Howard's lead role in this national drama as proof that immigration is a hang-up for conservatives only. Labor also echoed the Sydney–Melbourne two-step on race. In July 2002, in the same week of the so-called racism report, the gang-rape trial in Sydney, and the triple murder in Melbourne, NSW Labor Premier Bob Carr and Victorian Labor Premier Steve Bracks engaged in a spat. The topic was population policy, the marquee under which fertility and immigration debates are being played out today. Carr called on Howard to help him restrict further immigration to Sydney, citing environmental pressures. If Howard had said the same thing, he would have been accused of playing a race card. But Carr was playing a green card, and said he was keen to send more immigrants to the rest of New South Wales. Bracks, a third-generation Australian — his Catholic grandparents migrated as children from Lebanon in the 1890s — replied that it was 'senseless to say that big cities like Sydney and Melbourne are not going to grow'.[7]

That Carr, politically correct to his bootstraps, would choose to be seen as anti-immigration in the very week that the Sydney media resumed its obsession with the gang rapes shows just how race-sensitive politics has become in that city. Here is an example of the electorate Carr was managing, as gleaned from the listeners who rang Sydney talkback radio on 11 July 2002, the day the university racism report was released. Talkback radio callers are not strictly representative of the wider community, because there is an inherent bias towards people who are at home and are angry enough to pick up the phone. This forum matters, though, because politicians allow themselves to be snagged by it. Twenty-two callers phoned in their views. They proved to be a vicious vignette of old Australia; more than half (15) expressed various degrees of anger towards Muslims. The punters were ably assisted by the shock jocks, who applauded their thoughts. Philip Clark, host of the 2GB drive-time show, opined that racism would be reduced if Muslim women were discouraged from wearing the veil. He said it was a 'symbol of oppression' for these women. A few minutes later, Clark had another person on the line who said 'Muslims needed to live in the twenty-first century — all other religions have moved with the times'. Best not tell the Amish in the United States. The quote of the day, however, came from 77-year-old Daphne:

> Daphne says there was less obesity when she was young; there was no McDonald's. Clark says 'get off the plastic food'. Daphne says she has travelled all over the world; the people

> were lovely everywhere except Saudi Arabia; the Muslims in Jerusalem were 'arrogant'. She says it is pathetic how these people live with no toilets, no water, no nothing; how can they expect to come over here and be given five-storey houses when they have never done anything but use the open ground; they're expecting a lot as far as we are concerned.

The following morning, the Prime Minister's favourite radio host, the opinionated Alan Jones, engaged a caller named Ron on the gang rapes:

> Ron says these boys should join the national service. He says he has a lot of regard for Lebanese people, but there are people who should never have been brought here. Jones says he is quite right.[8]

What is intriguing about this is that the gang rapists were Australian-born. To accept the logic of Jones's conversation, we should vet immigrants on the basis that their Australian-born children might one day become rapists.

The following year, in March 2003, New South Wales voters went to the polls as the nation prepared to go to war with Iraq. The year began with peace rallies. During the state election campaign, with the invasion of Iraq only days away, one of the main parties tested the views of voters in western Sydney. The discussion turned to asylum-seekers or, specifically, their children. What stunned party officials was that this carefully selected cross-section of the community had little sympathy for kids still in detention or, more troublingly, those who had drowned trying to get to Australia. That was the parents' fault, for putting their children on the boats in the first place, was how one source paraphrased the sentiment.

Sydney's race fear is out of proportion to the numbers

involved. In August 2001, the Lebanese-born made up 1 per cent of the city's population and 3 per cent of its total immigrants. Their brethren in the bush accounted for 0.1 per cent of the rest of New South Wales. All up, Sydney's Lebanese amounted to a mere speck of 52,000 in a city of 4 million — and many of them are Christian, not Muslim. They ranked fifth behind Sydney's English-born (151,000); Chinese (82,000); New Zealanders (82,000); and Vietnamese (61,000). They pale beside the Australians who are truly disconnected from the community, either through long-term unemployment or mental illness. Sydney and immigration is a case of mind over matter.

On the less-inflammatory question of whether the Lebanese community is being left behind, economically speaking, the evidence suggests they are no different from other new Australians before them. The suburb that received the highest number of immigrants between 1990 and 2001 — Fairfield in Sydney's west — did not have Lebanese in its top five entrants. For the anti-immigration brigade, Fairfield is shorthand for the no-hoper postcode, an area so poor that it traps low-skilled immigrants into a cycle of exclusion. But even if we accept this dubious argument about Fairfield, the Lebanese are not part of it. The largest concentration of Lebanese can be found in neighbouring Bankstown. Even there, the Lebanese-born are not an enclave. Their ranks increased from 5 per cent to 6 per cent between the 1996 and 2001 censuses. The Vietnamese are moving in at a quicker pace, from 4 per cent to 6 per cent over the same period. The Lebanese of Bankstown have yet to surpass the English and Irish, who made up 7 per cent of the suburb in 1971. They are nowhere near the original non-English-speaking immigrant, the 14 per cent of the population in Marrickville that was Greek-born in 1971. Clearly, Sydney is not being inundated by Lebanese, which is counter to the perception being played out on planet talkback.

* * *

While we can't use electronic tags to track new Australians through time as we would, say, migrating birds, the census provides the next best approach. It involves checking the ethnic mix of indicative suburbs in Sydney and Melbourne, from 1961 to 2001. I use Marrickville and Richmond, the inner-city suburbs that took Greeks and Italians; Bankstown and Sunshine, the middle-ring suburbs that received Asians and Arabs; and, finally, Mosman and Camberwell, the wealthy suburbs where many Australians aspire to trade up to. In theory, there should be a rapid turnover from immigrant to high-income postcode. It is only when an ethnic group remains stuck in the same low-income suburb for more than a generation that Australians should worry.

Greek–Australians are the barometer of integration. By today's standards, they formed ghettoes in Marrickville and Richmond. In 1971, they comprised 14 and 20 per cent of these respective suburbs. Imagine what the shock jocks would have made of this had they been around then? Of course, Greeks became good Australians. They left the inner city for leafier addresses, a move that proved to be a blunder for some, given the inner-city property boom they missed out on in the 1990s. But we digress.

What is instructive is how many years it took the Greeks to change suburbs. Here we find only a subtle distinction between Sydney and Melbourne. The Greeks of Marrickville did not dominate as they had in Richmond, but they lingered longer. It wasn't until 1996 that the Vietnamese-born replaced the Greek-born as the top immigrant group in Marrickville — 6 per cent compared to 5 per cent. This was five years later than in Richmond where, in 1991, Vietnamese were 10 per cent and Greeks 6 per cent. The good news is that the Vietnamese departed more quickly than the Greeks. In Marrickville, the Vietnamese share of the population fell to 4 per cent in August 2001, placing them second behind the British and Irish. In Richmond, it was 7 per cent, a near-halving in ten years. On this score, at least, Vietnamese can be said to be the new Greeks. The middle-ring suburbs, Bankstown and Sunshine, can only be judged in a decade from now. But what we know already is that the concentration of newer arrivals here will never match the first immigrant waves to the inner cities.

The final pieces in the puzzle are the high-income suburbs, the neighbourhoods that are the last stop in the journey. Alas, Mosman remains out of reach to the overseas-born. Its top three foreign sources of ratepayers have not changed since 1971: the United Kingdom and Ireland, New Zealand, and the United Stares. This says more about Mosman, the first suburb in Australia to record a median house price above $1 million, than it does about the success of non-English-speaking immigration. But Camberwell, home of Peter Costello, had Greeks and Italians ranked second and third behind the British and Irish between 1971 and 1996, albeit at less than 2 per cent each. The Chinese surpassed both in August 2001. Upward immigrant mobility occurs more readily in Melbourne than in Sydney. But the same observation can be made about the local-born. Melbourne has more home owners generally than Sydney, and a smaller gap between rich and poor. The difference is a matter of degrees, not of substance. Sydney should come closer to the outlook of Melbourne with time.

There is one more area worth visiting, though, to see how immigration does work, even in Sydney. Howard's federal electorate of Bennelong, the nation's nineteenth most wealthy, in Sydney's inner north, boasts twice as many Asian-born constituents as Costello's seat of Higgins, the nation's seventh most wealthy, in Melbourne's latte-quaffing, cosmopolitan east.

Almost one in five (18 per cent) of Bennelong's residents are Asian-born, many of them Chinese. Camberwell, in the heart of Higgins, has a total Asian-born population of 9 per cent. The Asian-born are, to borrow a phrase from Hanson, swamping Bennelong. This is proof that immigration in Sydney is following Melbourne's lead on integration, rather than becoming the nightmare that Hanson warned of. Another encouraging number from Bennelong is the Lebanese-born, who approach 3 per cent of the population, a Bankstown-type level, and double the Sydney-wide result. On these numbers, Middle Eastern immigrants are on the same path to the middle class as the Asians and continental Europeans before them.

Unfortunately, the well-off in Sydney can be, well, put off by over-achieving immigrants. The Sydney rich had their own version of the Lebanese-gang scare after the 2001 election: the Asian-genius scare. Sydney's broadsheet press began debating the class-topping marks that Asian–Australian students earned at the selective public school Sydney Boys High — brother institution of Melbourne Boys High. The story began with a remark in 2002's first edition of the Sydney Boys High old boys' magazine, the *High Bulletin*, that the year-seven intake was '90 per cent Asian'. This statistic was subsequently shown to be false. Undaunted by the furore, the school moved to change its entry criteria. It came up with a plan to create a superstudent who would have to pass a test of character and show educational competence. Two of the additional hurdles to clear were that the new boys had to be sporty and civic-minded. Just thirty of the 180 students entering year seven would be chosen in this way. The school gave the new elite a suitably impenetrable bureaucratic title: the 'ethos enhancement group'.[9]

The subtext was that successful Asian–Australian students were not suiting up to play rugby union or any of the other contact sports that are supposed to transform boys into men. This is a big deal at Sydney Boys High, because if they didn't have enough students prepared to join the rugby league and union teams the public school risks losing its ticket to compete with the moneyed private schools. How do we know there was a sporting edge to this race play? Howard was prepared to speak out at the time. In April 2002, he told me he didn't agree with changing the rules. 'You either have a selective high school or you don't.' But Howard added, in his bet-each-way fashion:

> It is true that some groups don't participate as much in sport as others. That's an observation that has been made to me about some schools in my electorate.

Hold that thought for a moment, while we consider a B-grade movie twist to the tale of Sydney Boys High. One of the old boys responsible for drafting the new selection procedure was Marcus Einfeld, a former human rights commissioner. Howard and Einfeld were friends as Sydney law students in the late 1950s and early 1960s. But they fell out in 1988 when Howard wanted to slow the rate of Asian immigration, and Einfeld disowned him. Howard was stung by the inference of racism in Einfeld's rebuke. Howard would have appreciated the irony of Einfeld being incorrectly lumped with those who wanted to slow the rate of Asian intelligence at Sydney Boys High.

Whichever way you cut it, this was a very Sydney double-cross of Asian–Australians. In the 1980s and into the 1990s, the worry was that the 'yellow' would drain the welfare budget. But once Asian offspring proved the opposite, the complaint was that they were too smart. The sporting angle was a red herring. Boys of all backgrounds are less likely than twenty years ago to play either rugby code or AFL in the cities because high school has generally become more competitive, academically speaking.

Melbourne Boys High has had the same problem in fielding AFL teams as Sydney Boys High has with league and union. Kate Legge wrote in an article for the *Australian* in June 2003 that Melbourne Boys High once boasted '12 to 16 AFL teams in its annual contests with private schools, but now struggles to field eight'. That story barely raised a ripple in Melbourne, the home of the Australian Football League. It was only in inner-city Sydney that this unremarkable sign of a less-macho Australia was deemed worthy of a role in a wider race drama.

In the late 1960s, when Malcolm Fraser was briefly education minister in John Gorton's coalition government, he received about 200 letters a week complaining about Asian–Australian students in schools. A former Liberal colleague quoted Fraser as saying:

> The interesting thing is that 190 of those letters would come from affluent suburbs in Sydney and the rest from all over Australia. There was very heavy anti-Asian student bias in affluent suburbs, not in the poorer suburbs. In the poorer suburbs, they were less conscious that there might be some competition.

* * *

The childish Sydney–Melbourne rivalry is not what it once was. Long ago, the mutually assured petulance between cities forced the nation's founders to redraw the map. A third city, Canberra, was invented to serve as Australia's capital, the nation's only substantial inland settlement, 300 kilometres west of Sydney and 700 kilometres north of Melbourne.

One of the most amusing expressions of the Sydney versus Melbourne rivalry happened when John F. Kennedy was assassinated at the end of 1963. To the Sydneysider, the banner headline 'Kennedy Shot' referred to the US president. To many Melburnians, it was misread as the then local king of television, Graham Kennedy. The biographer of the latter Kennedy, Graeme Blundell, related the urban myth as follows:

> The day John F. Kennedy was assassinated in 1963, a passenger said to a Melbourne taxi driver, 'Pity about Kennedy being shot'. Without pause, the driver replied, 'Yeah, but it will give Bert Newton a chance.'[10]

It is, however, nonsense to talk about a big-city feud today. Any sense of contest between Melbourne and Sydney ended in the second half of the 1990s, when more Sydneysiders moved to Melbourne to live than vice versa. When the Sydneysiders landed, they found Melburnians had acquired an obsession with property prices. Yet stratospheric house prices in Melbourne have not translated to a Sydney vision of national identity. Howard was the first Sydney-born Liberal to win a federal election. By the time he had won three elections in a row in 2001, it was clear even to his critics that he knew what made the electorate tick. Yet Melbourne, the city that spawned the Liberal Party, rejected Howard each time. In fact, Victoria was the only mainland state to deliver a majority two-party preferred vote to Labor in the 1996, 1998, and 2001 elections.[11] It was also the one state to show the least fascination with One Nation. Whatever one thinks of Howard's mix of economically radical and socially reactive policies, they didn't resonate as loudly in Melbourne as they did elsewhere in Australia.

Before the *Tampa* united government MPs behind Howard, the nation saw Liberals divide on city lines in the first two big cultural wars of the new millennium. Sydney-born Howard was pitted against Melbourne-born Costello on the issues of the republic and a symbolic gesture for indigenous reconciliation. Howard was against both; Costello was for. As far as their home states went on the question of an Australian head of state, both politicians got it right. New South Wales had only fifteen out of its 50 federal electorates voting for the republic in 1999. Victoria, by contrast, secured a majority of 'yes' seats — eighteen out of 37 — but fell just short of a majority vote overall. Howard's Bennelong and Costello's Higgins electorates were both strongly for the republic (the 'yes' votes were 54.62 per cent and 63.66 per cent respectively). A large number of people in both electorates also marched for reconciliation in 2000. Howard avoided both events. He advised Costello not to join the throng on the Sydney Harbour Bridge in May, but did let him march in Melbourne later that year. This would suggest that high-income constituents in Sydney and Melbourne share common values. However, the 2001 federal election proved the reverse: Sydneysiders, both rich and poor, were more supportive of the war on boat people than Melburnians.

The way to measure this is to check the swings. The expectation going into the 2001 election was that those who voted for the republic and reconciliation in Sydney and Melbourne would swing, for the third time, against the Howard government on refugees. In fact, the opposite occurred. In Sydney, instead of recording a protest vote against the government, these republican and reconciliation seats swung to the government. It was only in Melbourne that a backlash could be detected. In Bennelong, the vote for Howard, after the distribution of preferences, increased by 2.47 per cent. In Higgins, the vote for Costello fell by 1.23 per cent. As a Costello supporter conceded immediately after the election:

> I have got no doubt there's a protest vote against us from Liberal supporters in Melbourne. Victoria has always been far

> more sympathetic to migrants, far more opposed to One Nation, far more accommodating of, particularly, Greeks, Italians, and Jews in our community. In Sydney, it's Jonesy, it's Carr, it's Howard's home town. There is no genuine voice of moderation on any of those issues, and it's also a reaction to the alleged rapes by the ethnic gangs. I think they spend a lot of time grasping in Sydney, climbing over people.

That Howard, with a more ethnically diverse electorate than Costello, could boast a swing to him in 2001, says that Asian and even Middle Eastern residents of Sydney's wealth belt were not overly offended by his crackdown on asylum-seekers.

The increased support for Howard in Bennelong was mirrored in three other pro-republic Liberal seats in Sydney — Berowra, North Sydney, and Wentworth — and in all ten Labor 'yes' electorates in Sydney and Newcastle. Berowra, held by the then immigration minister, Philip Ruddock, swung 2.28 per cent towards the government; North Sydney, held by moderate Liberal and Tourism Minister Joe Hockey, improved by 0.55 per cent; and Wentworth was up 0.49 per cent. The only other Liberal seat to vote for the republic in 1999, Warringah, held by the then workplace relations minister and monarchist Tony Abbott, had a high-profile, pro-refugee independent, Peter Macdonald, running in 2001. Abbott won comfortably, despite earlier fears that he would be unseated on the PC vote. The Liberal republican electorates in Melbourne numbered six — one more than in Sydney — in the inner-east electorates of Deakin, Higgins, and Kooyong; and in the metropolitan Aston, Goldstein, and Menzies. The two seats nestled alongside Costello's Higgins also swung *against* the government in 2001 — Deakin was down 0.19 per cent, and Kooyong, held by pro-refugee small-l liberal Petro Georgiou, lost 0.45 per cent. The remaining three electorates, Aston, Goldstein, and Menzies, swung to the government. These seats have lower immigration populations that might account for the difference. The rebuffs to Costello and Georgiou didn't escape the attention of Liberal powerbrokers. As one said:

> You wouldn't find two people more sympathetic to certain causes than those two, and that's probably one of the reasons why some [Liberal supporters] felt they could send a message to Howard — these are very safe seats.

At the Labor end, the inner-city federal seats of Sydney and Melbourne also diverged. In the seat of Sydney, the swing to the Liberals was 4.72 per cent. In the seat of Melbourne, it was 1.71 per cent, which was just below the national result of 1.87 per cent. Clearly, the well-off in Sydney had a different take on refugees than their cashed-up counterparts in Melbourne. This is not to infer prejudice; rather, it was the absence of an obvious protest vote that suggested Sydneysiders were less fussed than Melburnians when Howard shook his fist at the boat people.

* * *

The toffy end of town in Sydney is more self-centred than in Melbourne, another explanation for why the two cities can vary on race. Sydney's elite has less in common with the common folk. Just count the millionaires: three in every four taxpayers who declared $1 million-plus in income to the Australian Taxation Office in 1999–2000 were from Sydney. The nation has 22 super-rich postcodes, with 20 or more residents on taxable incomes above seven figures. Sydney was home to seventeen of the 22, Melbourne a mere four, and Perth one.[12]

The skewing of Sydney can be seen in the distribution of its breadwinners. New South Wales accounts for 34 per cent of the

Australian economy, but in August 2001 it boasted 41 per cent of the nation's high-income earners (on more than $78,000 a year), and 37 per cent of its middle-income earners ($52,000 to $71,999). Melbourne, in contrast, was in sync at each point: Victoria's 25 per cent of Australia's gross domestic product was matched by 25 per cent of the nation's well-off; 24 per cent of its middle class; and 25 per cent of its battlers (earning $20,800 to $51,999).[13] No wonder immigrants chase the lucre of Sydney, but find the more laid-back Melbourne gives them a better chance of feeling like an Australian. There is more room to breathe in Melbourne than in Sydney, the roads are less congested, and the public transport system is nimble by comparison: it runs late, as opposed to not at all. In Sydney — rich, poor, immigrant, or 'white' — you are more likely to agree that the door should be shut on any new entrants. The calculation is basic. The Sydneysider doesn't want another wealthy bidder to compete with at an inner-city auction, nor another welfare bludger to contend with at a western suburbs dole queue.

It is tempting here to write off Sydney as un-Australian in its attitudes to immigration. That, however, would assume that Sydney is irredeemable, that it has become a city permanently divided on income and united in intolerance. Although feedback from voters in the western suburbs two years after the *Tampa* is a serious concern, as witnessed in the private NSW state polling in early 2003, we should treat it with caution. Also, it would be hypocritical to argue that immigrants are no different, but that Sydneysiders are. Attitudes in Sydney have been shaped by the city's housing market. One argument that the NSW government runs is that Sydney simply can't fit in any more people. This is disingenuous. Between 1996 and 2001, Sydney lost residents to all city and country areas in the nation with the exception of Adelaide, Hobart, and Canberra. Melbourne, in contrast, picked up extra citizens from all parts, both city and bush: New South

Wales, South Australia, Western Australia, Tasmania, Canberra, and the Northern Territory. These people flows suggest that the problem in Sydney is not immigrants, but something more fundamental: it has become a city too expensive for many to live in.

Sydney is not a lost cause. In 2003, a familiar face defied the exodus by moving into the city's new-money harbourside address of Sylvania Waters, home of the nation's first family of reality television, Noeline Baker and Laurie Donaher. It was Pauline Hanson, the siren of old Australia. She figured she was a certainty to secure a spot in the NSW upper house. Indeed, her former political partner David Oldfield had done so in 1999. A strange thing happened on the way to her planned resurrection as a NSW state politician: the punters were happy to leave Hanson buried. She was beaten for the final place in the NSW parliament by another single-issue politician, John Tingle of the Shooters Party. One of the ironies here is that it was the Howard government's gun-law reforms in 1996 that gave Hanson and her former One Nation Party its first big break.

Sydney's instinct on race may be darker than Melbourne's. Yet it is discerning enough to have eventually ignored Hanson. In seven short years after she started her anti-immigration debate, Hanson could not claim even the 2 per cent of the popular vote she needed to call herself a New South Wales parliamentarian.

I'D LIKE TO ORDER SOME TAKE-AWAY PLEASE – THE WIFE'S GOT ANOTHER B.A. IN THE OVEN...

CHAPTER FOUR

The Economics of Motherhood

> 'In the last couple of years, the government has boasted about increasing the number of women in the work force. Rather than something to be proud of, I feel that this is something of which we should be ashamed.'
> —Paul Keating, maiden speech to parliament, 1970

THE PATHFINDERS OF NEW AUSTRALIA began school in 1969, when a young fogey named Paul Keating was elected to federal parliament. Their final year at high school, in 1981, marked the last occasion that the economy grew under the old order of protection. As these first new Australians entered university the following year, the nation sunk into its worst recession since the great depression. The tertiary students of the early 1980s were amongst the most pessimistic outside a war because they had no reason to believe that decent jobs awaited them on graduation. What is more remarkable about this group, though, is its make-up. In 1982, there were more women than men under twenty enrolled in higher education. In each year after, women outnumbered men.[1] This was the start of Generation W's winning streak.

Keating's class grew up much faster than he had done. In 1969, when he was aged 25 and they were five, Keating commenced his career with an axe to grind as an MP in Gough

Whitlam's Labor opposition. The member for Blaxland in Sydney's west used his maiden speech to parliament to ridicule John Gorton's coalition government for allowing women to sneak out of the kitchen:

> Husbands have been forced to send their wives to work in order to provide the necessities of life. Young mothers have been forced out of their homes by economic pressure.

Keating was not a women's libber: 'Is this government … doing anything to put the working wife back in her home? It is not. It engages in a lot of claptrap'. Nor was he pro-immigrant: 'It is time we considered the enormous cost of bringing migrants to this country … After all, the best migrant is the infant Australian.' How amusing then, that the primary school children of 1969 reached adulthood at the same time that Keating began constructing an economy that was tailored for them. The coincidence is so remarkable that it seems preordained. Keating's logic was to force Australia to compete in a world that placed greater value on what was in our heads than what we could dig out of the ground. Enter the women and the children of immigrants that Keating had seen barely twenty years earlier as un-Australian.

Generation W united chromosomes X and Y in the work force by their qualifications. Women, in particular, doubled the supply of educated workers when the economy needed them the most. Their timing could not have been more exquisite for Keating. Without them, Australia would have operated on half the required horsepower, and would have flunked the test of globalisation in the 1980s and 1990s. Women not only had the marks at school, they were less likely to be in trade unions and were more willing to take on part-time jobs — two of the many preconditions for running a post-protection economy. The competitive edge enjoyed by women also applied at the bottom of the income ladder. This reveals a less redeeming part of the labour market, where employers prefer to hire older workers on a casual basis and at minimal cost.

It is easy to forget how quickly Australia metamorphosed, because we take the Keating–Howard economy for granted today. In 1983, Bob Hawke's Labor government unpegged the Australian dollar with no real confidence. Keating, then the new kid treasurer, was especially nervous about handing over control of the currency to the whim of foreigners. However, once it was clear that the sky wouldn't fall in, Keating swung from nervous passenger to confident pilot. The next year — as the first of the pupils of 1969 completed their free university degrees — the old banking system was put to the sword. Interest-rate ceilings were removed, and competition was introduced which, by the mid-1990s, placed a mortgage, a credit card, and a frequent-flyer program within reach of the average worker.

The women of new Australia had the advantage of being shielded, in the best sense of the word, from the previous era of tariffs. They didn't have jobs when work was protected, so they were less likely to be caught working in areas that the Keating–Howard economy deemed redundant over the course of the 1980s and 1990s. And they had less to lose at the end of the 1980s, when restructuring and another recession wiped out hundreds of thousands of positions in the manufacturing sector. This allowed women to achieve a consistently lower rate of unemployment than men in the 1990s and into the new millennium.

⁂ ⁂ ⁂

In August 2001, I interviewed some of the children of new Australia to see how they were getting along. I picked a sample that had gone to Ringwood High School, which is public, co-ed, and sits roughly in the middle of Victoria's year-twelve league tables. This group completed their higher school certificates (HSC) in 1981, which makes them a telling case-study of the intake that confirmed the shift from men to women at university in 1982.

As bland as bath water, suburbs such as Ringwood, in Melbourne's eastern suburbs, some 30 kilometres from the city centre, housed Robert Menzies' forgotten people in the 1950s. This is not the new Australia of the inner city that is either demonised or deified, depending on the spin of the pundit. It is the middle Australia that John Howard still wants to relate to. Ringwood is in the marginal federal Liberal electorate of Deakin, which adjoins Aston — the place where, at a by-election a month earlier in July 2001, Howard won against the odds after the GST gave him his worst run of polling numbers as prime minister. I chose the sons and daughters of old Australia because they are above suspicion of bias. They are the least controversial collection of people in the work–family argument because, unlike many experts, they live the lives we are talking about. I didn't ask them what they thought about the hot topics of the day, but rather to describe their lives.

One in four (eighteen of the 72) of Ringwood High's 1981 HSC year agreed to tell their stories to me at the *Australian*. Once we got talking, they couldn't stop, which is a good thing, of course. Every person interviewed went on to achieve some form of tertiary qualification — a pointer that prosperity has gone mainstream. Their circumstances will no doubt have changed since we spoke. However, in keeping with one of the themes of this book, I concentrate here on their experiences up to August 2001.

The dilemma of the well-educated generation is, simply, life. The one original act most of us have to offer to the world — the creation of life — is increasingly being associated with loss: loss of freedom, loss of opportunity, and loss of income. It is not the life before children that parents long for, but a better sense of how to manage the new life they have. Having raised the expectations of most women by giving them a career before motherhood, society has yet to work out how to facilitate their divergent demands once babies arrive.

Of our Ringwood class, twelve of the 18 were women, eleven of whom were mothers by August 2001, while the other was happily single. Of the six men, five were fathers, while the other was gay. A minority of the women with children — five of the 11 — chose to be full-time mothers. However, two of this group of five said they would take flexible jobs if they were available. Another two of the stay-at-home mothers tried part-time work, but it didn't work out. The majority — six of the 11 mothers — returned to employment when their children were young, with four taking full-time jobs.

Only one of the five Ringwood High fathers had a stay-at-home wife. Two of the five could claim the tag of 'SNAG dad' as they shared the job of raising the children — which makes these men unrepresentative of fathers generally. Aside from that minor glitch, the Ringwood class of 1981 fits in with the census taken in August 2001, which showed that 51 per cent of mothers in two-parent families were back at work when their youngest child was aged one to two years.

* * *

Lisa nailed the mixed emotions of Generation W:

> My mother once said she did not feel the same frustration with parenthood that I was experiencing because she never had a career or skills or knowledge that were being lost the longer she stayed away.

Lisa married bank executive Gerry in 1989. They waited seven years before starting a family. By that time, she was 31 and a lecturer at Perth Central TAFE. She was offered a part-time position when the first of her three sons, Darcy, was eight months old.

> I combined evening lectures with non-lecturing work that I could do at home, so my husband and I could still care for our son without needing to use child care. It was much more difficult than I anticipated.

It took one semester for Lisa to decide she should drop work and concentrate on motherhood, which she has not regretted.

> My parents were much younger than us. They had not established careers or paid off their mortgage. These were things that were very important to my husband and I. We wanted to have financial security and to have felt as though we had achieved just a few of our dreams before our life was so dramatically changed by having children. I wonder sometimes whether we actually created our own frustrations by making such a contrast between our two lives — BC and AC, before children and after children.

Lisa was slightly ahead of her time in one respect. The age at which she began motherhood in 1989 — 31 years — became the national median for married women in 2001. For unmarried mothers, it was 26 years. Twenty years earlier, when the 1981 year were swotting for their HSC exams, the median age of motherhood was 27 years for married women, and 22 years for those who weren't.[2]

⁂ ⁂ ⁂

Predominantly 'white', Ringwood is the quarter-acre block from central casting, where people still like to raise families. Many have remained in the area. Others crossed the Yarra River to inner-city Melbourne. The most remarkable thing about these families is the absence of rancour. The rift that politicians, academics, and the media tell us exists between working and stay-at-home mothers did not appear among the Ringwood alumni. The most common sentence uttered by parents was that their choice should not be seen as reflecting on anyone else's. This should not be that great a surprise. These people not only understood each other; they had been in each other's shoes. Many of the working mothers had tried to stay at home, and many of the stay-at-homes had gone to work.

Nevertheless, many sensed that society was judging them unfairly. As one said: 'There was all sorts of subtle pressure in the media about how to be a mum. The idea of going back to work is akin to one of the worst crimes in society.' Another said: 'I'm not ashamed about staying at home, but you do feel second-class about your choice. You feel as if you have betrayed the cause a bit.' The dichotomy is that politicians and the media see working and staying at home as mutually exclusive concepts, as if people in those categories are somehow from different dimensions. But what they achieve, instead, is a double-barrelled insult. They miscast the majority of families whose lives are more complex and less contentious than the typecasts. In doing so, they make people feel inferior.

One of the highest achievers from Ringwood, Belinda faced motherhood wondering whether she might enjoy it on a full-time basis. But she didn't feel comfortable at home, and quickly resumed full-time work as a law professor at the University of Melbourne:

> I was really surprised that I wanted to go back. It wasn't anything to do with how much I love the baby because I love my child [Amy, born January 1998]. But I found it quite difficult, that loss of autonomy and lack of interaction. I had always been a very organised person and suddenly I just couldn't organise my life in the same way at all. It would be 12 o'clock and I would be sitting in my dressing-gown a few times, and I would think: 'This is not me.' It was better for me to go back to work. That's not any sort of comment on what suits other people.

Belinda returned to work full-time when Amy was six months old. She is more typical than she realises. In 2001, 11 per cent of mothers in two-parent families resumed full-time work before their youngest child's first birthday, and 24 per cent were full-time with a child aged one to two years. Her husband, Gerry, is a partner in a top-end-of-town law firm. The price for Belinda keeping her career has been to employ a full-time nanny. She splits the cost with her sister, who has a young boy. It helps that the siblings live in the neighbouring inner-city suburbs of North Carlton and Northcote. However, there is not much left of Belinda's salary after all these bills are paid.

This is another common theme from Ringwood. Many work not so much for the money, but to stay connected with their professions. Otherwise, they worry that they will be left behind. The reality of the two-income society is that the second job is often a device to remain qualified, not an indulgence to help fund a holiday to Noosa.

* * *

Having an educated choice — a career before the children arrive — does not take economics out of the equation. Rather, it reinforces it. Another important lesson from Ringwood is that income still dictates whose life undergoes the greatest change. It is the one who was earning less before the children came, which means the mother in most examples. The income deficit between men and women is a sticking point for society generally. One of three things can happen from here on: women can achieve true pay equality, which would remove the market-induced bias that presently discourages fathers from sharing the load in raising children; women can deliberately marry down by finding men who will serve as their 'wives'; or we can continue with the present mess, which satisfies neither women nor men.

From one angle, the saga of our sagging birth rate is simply about the pill. The year the nation stopped making enough babies to replace the population was 1976, when most mothers were still at home with a youngest child aged 6–13 years. But Generation W has accelerated the decline in fertility by dint of its education. The higher a woman's income, the fewer children she has. Women on the bottom two rungs of the income ladder still delivered the requisite 2.1 babies on average in 2002. It is the better-paid who set the record low birth-rates.

Two of the 16 Ringwood classmates who had had children switched traditional roles, leaving the father as chief carer and the mother as breadwinner. Economics ruled in both examples. Geoff offers a neat summary, and a surprise connection to the pop culture of Generation W. He became a stay-at-home dad initially because his wife was earning more. You may remember his face. He joined the cast of 'Neighbours' in 1985, alongside Kylie, Guy Pearce, and Jason Donovan. Later, he was the slick-haired security guard in *The Wog Boy*. Geoff married in 1989. His priorities changed in 1992 when children and a mortgage in Coburg, in Melbourne's inner north, arrived:

> My wife Kath went back to work [as a district nurse] three or four months after the twins [Alex and Sophie] were born. We just simply had to get a steady income. She has worked three days a week since.

It was Geoff who had to put his career on hold for the first two years, taking only small roles, before he returned to full-time acting and writing. 'It didn't bring out the feminine side in me; it brought out the grumpy side', he says, only half-joking. 'I just suddenly felt like life was finished and, combined with sleep deprivation, you just become zombie-like.' In August 2001, Geoff and Kath managed the task of rearing the children in thirds, between father, mother, and childcare.

Of the remaining four of the five fathers from Ringwood, one had already cut his hours to help share the job of parenting, while the other three were in the process of becoming pseudo-SNAGs — translation, they intended to spend more time with their children.

⁂ ⁂ ⁂

Brian, the sixth man from Ringwood, is gay. His balancing act is equally universal — between work and home life. His choices, like those of his classmates, have been individual. Brian had, as he says, 'a very clichéd coming out' after leaving high school. He got a job at a restaurant, bought a car, and discovered that Melbourne had a night life. Then he became an accountant:

> I question now why I decided to do accounting for ten years. I did enjoy it when I was working for corporates, don't get me wrong, but I am not interested in doing it now.

His rethink was prompted by a serious illness in the mid-1990s.

Brian was diagnosed with HIV. 'I was very sick twice. I felt like I actually would die. But I am much better now.'

Brian dropped the party scene of St Kilda for an eight-hectare property in Flowerdale, 90 minutes from Melbourne. The plan was to grow wildflowers to export to Japan:

> I think life-threatening illness forces those types of changes. I think that if you haven't had any situations like that in twenty years, you would be on the same path, and that's okay. In 1981, a lot of the 1960s and 1970s activism through unis and gay liberation had happened so I feel like I haven't had to fight for a cause. We finished school and the world was pretty well opened up. It wasn't like we really had to grapple with it.

The politicians, academics, and pundits who place men and women in camps are wasting their biases. Life was never that simple to begin with. Now the economy, and the society it serves, is more diverse than ever, and people are moving more quickly than experts can find labels for them. No sooner do we put a parent in category A than they switch to B then C, sometimes over the course of one year. It's called life, and those who don't get it should perhaps get one of their own.

⁂ ⁂ ⁂

One of the shocks in the 2001 census was how quickly the single-income family was shrinking. In 1986, the one-breadwinner model was the experience of 40 per cent of all young families with children aged 0–5 years. Back then, two-income families with the father working full-time and the mother working either part-time or full-time were 10 percentage points behind. Some 15 years later, in August 2001, the roles had been reversed. The typical two-income family had risen to 35 per cent, while the traditional single-income family had slipped to 28 per cent. These figures do not account for the combinations of a breadwinner on part-time hours, both parents unemployed, or single-parent households.[3] Anyone pretending to place one example above the other is frankly playing the hand of a narrow mind.

I remember a school buddy once sledged me because my parents were poor. Like olive skin, a working-class background is a badge of honour today. Both my father and mother worked, Dad as a railway signalman and Mum in various cleaning and factory jobs. The father of the boy who baited me about our lack of income was in the professional class: his mother, from memory, was a full-time mum.

My family hit the working-class jackpot in the mid-1970s when my mother became head cleaner at the long-demolished Hoyts Malvern cinema. At the age of ten — the year I absorbed that grand final in the tree — I helped Mum at work. We were a one-broom outfit then, because she didn't dare tell the boss that she was sneaking in child labour. I scooped what junk I could from under the seats by hand. My mother skipped behind me, sweeping the refuse into a plastic bin. I went formally on the payroll in my early teens, when I earned the right to carry my own broom. Sprucing up a cinema is a classic Sisyphean situation: a chore doomed to mindless repetition. We'd get the lower level ready for the morning session, then the patrons would meander into their chairs. I'd finish the top half by torchlight as the first screening flickered below. By early afternoon, both tiers were jammed with Jaffas, popcorn, and melted choc tops and, occasionally, toe-nail clippings. But I didn't mind groundhog garbage day as this was my first wad of pocket money, plus a free seat at any movie I wanted to see, from the *Star Wars* trilogy to *The Last Waltz*.

Immigrant couples worked in the 1950s, 1960s, and 1970s,

just as they do today. Of course, it helped that they had extended families to pitch in with childminding. When RMIT professor Belinda Probert interviewed women of all backgrounds to compare attitudes in the 1950s with today, she found that the single-income family was a 'peculiar postwar phenomenon' restricted to Australian-born mothers, regardless of education and income.[4] The typical two-income family today reflects a practical alignment of old and new Australia. Anglo-Celtic families now feel they need to work as hard as immigrants do to stay ahead. Welcome to globalisation.

Whether this is what people want is another matter, but it should no longer be the role of government to trip-wire the tax system to facilitate the return of women to the kitchen at the expense of those who want to and those who have to work. Baby bonuses don't work anyway; they merely provide martini money for the well-paid. The contradiction of conservative politics is that it abhors the notion of nanny-state welfare — the handouts that keep sole parents trapped at home in poverty. Yet it still preaches middle-class welfare to encourage mothers with well-off husbands to raise children.

The solution is less complicated than it seems. First, governments must find a way to neutralise any bias in its family payments system. That means real income-tax reform, not an increase in handouts. At the moment, we live in a strange half-world where a worker on average earnings of just under $50,000 a year is on the cusp of paying the tax rates meant for high-income earners. The Howard government has allowed itself to be snookered here because it fears the battlers won't tolerate a cut to the top personal tax rates of 42 and 47 cents in the dollar. But each year the bracket creeps up to bring the battler closer to those thresholds, and so does the political pressure for corrective measures. A little understood but explosive part of Howard's taxation system is that the battlers are penalised when the mother decides to go back to work. Each extra dollar she earns costs her between 60 cents and 80 cents in reduced family-payment benefits and increased taxes. This is before out-of-pocket expenses such as child care and transport. Yet the census shows that women work anyway. Howard doesn't pay them enough to keep them at home, and takes too much from them when they go back to the office. This is an unsustainable state of affairs for a working nation with an ageing population.

Participants in the work–family debate have agonised about how to make payments equal. Sorry, chaps, but that is like arguing over which passenger should be freed first from a car wreck. The problem begins with the tax scales, not the handouts that are attached to them. Lower personal tax-rates are the cleanest way to reduce the tax traps that apply to women when they move back to work. Remove that disincentive by choosing tax cuts ahead of middle-class welfare, and there is the potential to liberate billions in the budget. Once that is done, it becomes much easier for governments to deliver what assistance it figures is necessary for women who stay at home without compromising the position of working mothers.

Beyond tax, there is a very simple social-policy shift that should be contemplated. Governments at all levels must accept the reality that women return to work long before their children reach primary school. By bringing forward pre-school to the age of, say, two years, families would be given the choice to avoid child care. Pre-school should, of course, be optional, because it is not the state's role to take toddlers away from stay-at-home mothers. The trick here is to maximise the options for those who want to, have to, or feel they need to work. From there, governments should leave the rest to the market and to individual families.

The educated generation of women is acquiring leverage in the workplace that it may not yet appreciate. The balance of power between professional worker and employer is tilting towards the former as the nation ages. Put simply, there won't be another generation of fresh meat to follow this one — the women and the children of immigrants who entered the workforce for the first time in the 1980s and 1990s. So the next batch of employers will face a shrinking supply of qualified men, women, and immigrants generally, and they will need to treat their staff with more sensitivity to keep them.

* * *

Howard waited until his eighth year as prime minister before officially welcoming the two-income family to his political world. He nominated policemen and part-time sales assistants as his new benchmark for the battlers: 'We are not living in a society where the norm is two full-time highly paid professionals,' he said. '[That is] an unduly elitist paradigm.'[5]

Well, it depends on what sort of couple we are talking about. Those with children are more likely to fit with Howard's new 1.5 incomes' stereotype. Those without children, though, are more likely to be on two full-time incomes.

So let's pose one more trick question. Which is the mainstream couple — the one with young children, or the one without? The 1996 census told us what sort of Australia Keating left for Howard. There were a little over 1.6 million couples with children aged fourteen or under; the couples without children numbered just 16,000 fewer. By August 2001, they had swapped places. Couples without children were now almost 1.8 million strong; those with children aged fourteen or under settled at 1.6 million. The difference now was ten times the other way at 163,000.[6] The childless generation is the real mainstream couple. Yet baby boomers think this is a cause for embarrassment.

The population debate is, in essence, absurd. First, it assumes that having children later is a problem. Second, it implies that the solution is to encourage women to get pregnant before they establish financial independence through their careers. This would be a bizarre command for a libertarian and capitalist nation to issue.

The decision on whether, when, or not to have children is as personal as the decisions mothers make about whether, when, or not to go back to work. It is no one else's business. But politicians and the press seem more interested in playing one person's life against another's. This is the culture of the guilt trip, which makes all women, be they childless, mothers at work, or at home, feel that someone out there disapproves. An example of this was seen in July 2002 when an ABC television journalist, Virginia Haussegger, wrote an opinion article about being childless. Her personal feelings prompted some women to offer their own experience as the sole answer, which is the antithesis of the balanced responses from Ringwood. Approaching 40, Haussegger confessed that she felt betrayed by women's lib:

> Angry that I was so foolish to take the word of my feminist mothers as gospel. Angry that I was daft enough to believe female fulfilment came with a leather briefcase.

Haussegger had chased the career that was her birthright as a modern woman. But she had left her run at motherhood too late, with her doctor advising her that IVF offered only a one-in-five chance of success:

> The point is that while encouraging women in the 1970s and 1980s to reach for the sky, none of our purple-clad, feminist mothers thought to tell us the truth about the biological clock. Our biological clock. The one that would eventually reach exploding point inside us.

Without meaning to, Haussegger caused divisions amongst women. Letters to editors across the nation either thanked her for speaking up or thundered that she was a spoilt brat who should grow up. Here is a sample of three letters to Melbourne's the *Age*, all from women, published in the week the opinion piece ran:

> Thank you for being brave enough to tell the truth, Virginia Haussegger. I fortunately did not have a blazing feminist mother and although I had career aspirations, I chose to stay at home and have my six children in an eight-year period ... There hasn't been one moment when I would have sent one of them back. They have enriched my life and taught me many lessons that I otherwise would have missed. And now, at 35, I'm considering what to do once they have all left home. Having children doesn't end your life, it is just the beginning.

> Virginia Haussegger, they say the first sign of maturity is when you stop blaming everything on your parents. Grow up. As for the biological clock, that concept didn't just drop out of the sky in 2002.

> Lately I've read several articles by women struggling to have it all — career, lifestyle, family. Could it be that the reason they struggle is because they lack the massive support relationship that most men have relied on for decades? These women lack a wife. It's strange that more women don't search for partners who are less career-minded than themselves.

One of the reasons the concepts of work and family are so hard for politicians to grapple with is the lack of an obvious majority view on the subject. Haussegger demonstrated the pitfalls: she was criticised for having a personal opinion about a contentious subject. The reaction, in the end, was not about her at all.

It reflected, instead, the disconnections of democracy.

* * *

If enough people lead comfortable lives, they earn the right to avoid getting involved in politics. The field is thus vacated to the most narrow-cast individuals of all: the party loyalist, the lobbyist, and the journalist. Those who write letters to newspapers do not sound like the people I interviewed from Ringwood. The latter understood that what they do in their lives is not a reflection on anyone else. But that's not how parliament or the media works. These institutions find it easier to deal with petty conflict than to discuss policy content. Unfortunately, some people believe them and write to newspapers or ring talkback radio programs. It becomes a self-fulfilling parroting of political spin, which convinces politicians they are on to something.

Of course, we could retreat to recreate the consensus of the stay-at-home 1950s, which is the cry we hear from time to time from old Australia. But no politician in his or her right (or left) mind would contemplate a return to our blue-collar past, as it would hobble two of the most important sections of the economy: women and immigrants. This would deny those in old Australia the opportunity of joining the middle class.

One mark of economic progress is to compare Howard's checklist of who is in and out of the middle class today with the checklist nominated by Robert Menzies in his defining 1942 radio broadcast, 'The Forgotten People'. The middle-class Australia that Menzies described was, on one level, more egalitarian. He included professionals in his definition of the centre. Yet the nation was also more snobbish. Menzies excluded trade unionists — 'the mass of unskilled people, almost invariably well-organised, and with their wages and conditions safeguarded by popular law':

> Salary earners, shopkeepers, skilled artisans, professional men and women, farmers and so on — these are, in the political and economic sense, the middle class.[7]

It is a mark of upward mobility in Australia that what was working class to Menzies is counted as middle class by Howard — his policeman is likely to be a trade unionist. And what was middle class, the professional worker, is now seen as elite. Howard sees no need, politically speaking, to worry about professionals because they are now more likely to vote Labor. The policeman, on the other hand, is part of the new conservative worker, the former Labor supporter who has acquired a stake, via a mortgage, in middle Australia. Nevertheless, the middle class remains, as Menzies said then, 'constantly in danger of being ground between' the top and the bottom. The majority of this category votes Labor. What bugs the left is the defection of the battlers in specific seats in New South Wales and Queensland. What troubles Howard is that his battlers need two incomes to get by.

It may not suit our Antipodean self-loathing to admit this, but the Australia of the banana republic 1980s became the boom regime of the 1990s. The economy grew faster than any other in the developed world — 3.4 per cent a year, after removing inflation, between 1990 and the start of 2002. Norway, whose flag the *Tampa* sailed under, and the United States were next, on 3 per cent each. As it happens, Australia and the United States (along with Ireland) are unique. They are the only first world economies to have increased their share of global production between 1980 and 2001 — the rest, including Japan, lost ground to the likes of China. What do Australia and the US have in common? They are the world's two most identifiable immigrant nations. Immigrants make Australians generally more prosperous, and the economy less likely to shrink because of low fertility rates. Don't take my word for it. Listen to the Governor of the Reserve Bank, Ian Macfarlane:

> Some people would discount our achievement by pointing out that a fair bit of our increase in share [of world output] was due to higher population growth resulting from higher levels of immigration. But that should be seen as a strength rather than a weakness if we are interested in which areas are growing and which are declining in relative importance. Also, it points to favourable developments in the future, as high-immigration countries are less susceptible to the strains imposed by an ageing population.[8]

We can put women back in the kitchen, and stop more immigrants from coming here, but that would return us to old Australia. If we are that keen to go back, remember that our wages and house prices would follow us down. Macfarlane points out, in another talk, that Australians tend to forget the relative poverty that existed in the so-called golden age of the 1950s, when Menzies ruled:

> For example, much of the post-war housing expansion into the new suburbs involved two-bedroom-one-bathroom houses and external toilets. Sealed roads, sewerage, and telephones came years later, along with much-improved living standards.[9]

A few months after this speech, a four-bedroom house in Balmain, in what was once Sydney's working-class inner west, sold for just under $1.3 million. The thirty-something woman who bought it, a lawyer, became known to her friends as Miss Outdoor Dunny — the property she had acquired still boasted its original, free-standing loo.

IT WAS THE REPUBLIC WE DIDN'T HAVE TO HAVE....
REFERENDUM

CHAPTER FIVE

Unfinished Business: the republic

'The biggest danger is producing a species of homogenised, white-bread politicians who fail, not because they are inadequate or lazy, but because their sameness will mean it will be impossible for them to represent the interests of their constituents.'
—Gary Gray, Labor Party national secretary, March 2000

THE THREE Rs of republic, reconciliation, and refugees distinguish new Australia from old, and city from bush. The assumption, shared by many politicians and political junkies, is that the closer you get to the CBD in each capital city the better is your education, the fatter is your salary and, thus, the more likely you are to be a triple-R subscriber. The further you go the other way, the more likely you are to recoil at the very idea of change.

At face value, the result of the republic referendum and public opinion polling on reconciliation and refugees suggest that roughly the same number of people line up in each 'yes' and 'no' camp. At the 1999 referendum, 45.13 per cent voted for a republic, while 54.87 per cent said no. Immediately after the Sydney 2000 Olympics, Newspoll found that 42 per cent of Australians favoured a formal apology to Australian Aboriginals for past mistreatment, while 51 per cent were against. The Newspoll taken in the first weekend of September 2001 after John Howard turned back the *Tampa* revealed that 47 per cent of the community wanted some or all asylum-seekers to be allowed to land on our shores, while 50 per cent wanted all boats turned away. A couple of weeks later, after the September 11 terror attacks on New York, Washington, and Pennsylvania, the pro-refugee score was 41 per cent, while anti-refugee sentiment had jumped to 56 per cent.[1] The symmetry in these results is misleading. To appreciate why, we must consider, one chapter at a time, the republic, reconciliation, refugees — and Howard, the politician who convinced the electorate to say 'no'. Despite the neatness of the figures, each debate saw a different group of voters engaged. Even Generation W did not behave consistently. Some were for and some were against, depending on which 'R' was in the headlight of public debate.

Forget for a moment which side of these arguments you are on, and consider the following question: how many Australians does it takes to change something? No, this isn't an Irish or Polish or public service joke. The minute Howard moves on, and either hands over to Peter Costello or loses an election to Labor, the republic debate will be revived and politicians will come under renewed pressure to advance the symbolic aspect of reconciliation. Refugees are another matter — there is precious little sympathy in the electorate for asylum-seekers at the moment.

Nations always outlast their leaders. That's the beauty of democracy. Howard's success in the cultural wars is temporary. Remember, he got the Asian immigration issue wrong and gave us Peter Hollingworth as governor-general; hardly a masterstroke to fortify the monarchy beyond the reign of Elizabeth II. Saying 'no' in 1999 and 2000 doesn't mean that the subjects of republic and reconciliation won't be raised again. New Australia has time on its side, and its numbers are rising. Obviously, many will turn conservative in their middle age, as many baby boomers have done. However, economic power tends to translate to political power, sooner or later. And ideas that seemed too radical one year can quickly return as mainstream the next.

Let's begin with the republic. By any measure, the November 1999 referendum was the most ridiculous ballot of its type. It was an oxymoron in its own category, the only moment in our history in which a prime minister put a question to the people *not* to change the constitution. Howard was asking the electorate to reject what opinion polls showed the majority wanted. In the eight years that Newspoll surveyed the community between 1994 and 2002, opposition to the general idea of an Australian republic never rose above 37 per cent. In August 1999, with the referendum a mere two months away, those in favour of a republic stood at 51 per cent, those against 35 per cent, and those uncommitted at 14 per cent. It was, of course, the particular model on offer that was rejected, not the aspiration for an Australian head of state.

Howard saved the Queen because republicans were split on the method of choosing a new figurehead. The republicans were like a couple too busy fighting over what to call the baby to get into bed to conceive it. The referendum had been trumpeted as a conscience debate. Liberal Party MPs were free to speak from the heart. However, this did not secure an open debate. There was a fissure in republican ranks based on personality, not principle, which destroyed any idea of an informed argument. The most senior Liberal to support the 'yes' vote was Costello. Peter Reith, the then industrial relations minister, was the highest-ranking republican to urge a 'no' vote. Reith said that 'no' would mean 'yes' down the track when a more radical model for electing a president would be put to the people.

Reith is an interesting character. In 1999, he told voters that his views supporting a directly elected president 'had been on the public record for years'. Those views, he said, were consistently held. Yet the public record shows he previously supported the monarchy — in a letter to the Queen, no less, published in Melbourne's *Herald Sun*. He also had previously argued for a minimalist republic, much like the one he told the electorate it should reject. All he could say when confronted with his earlier missive to Elizabeth II was: 'I was on the backbench then and I was writing pieces for various newspapers on the issues, so what?'[2] So what, indeed. In 1999, Reith fancied he could be the next prime minister, instead of Costello.

The Australian electorate is famously reluctant to tamper with the constitution, even when it has both main parties urging a 'yes' vote. The republican debate was unique in that the main combatants were not at the outset politicians, but private lobby groups: the Australian Republican Movement, and Australians for Constitutional Monarchy. The latter quickly dropped its advocacy for the Queen, and turned its publicity machine, instead, to something it knew it could sell: the idea that voters should reject the 'politicians' republic'. The discussion soon slipped into the quicksand of esoteric questions such as whether the governor-general was already the 'effective head of state'. The referendum never stood a chance, and was defeated by all six states. The margin in favour of the status quo was 1,137,763 votes. Yet there is more to the defeat than meets the eye.

When Newspoll ran a follow-up survey almost two years after the referendum, the result was 52 per cent for a republic, 35 per cent against, and 13 per cent on the fence. No one had changed their minds. This was in July 2001, on the eve of the *Tampa*. So Howard had not, in fact, saved the monarchy in perpetuity. The referendum did not mark a revival in support for the Queen and her heirs, the children whose dysfunctional relationships routinely grace the covers of checkout-counter celebrity magazines. All Howard achieved, aided by self-styled republicans such as his political ally Reith, was to temporarily transfer around 6–7 percentage points from the 'yes' to the 'no' side of the ballot paper. An Australian head of state is the no-brainer of the new millennium. There remains a majority for a republic ready to be tapped by a less cynical group of politicians.

The accepted wisdom is that the referendum offered a neat summation of our doughnut-shaped nation, where new Australia has carved out a cosmopolitan niche in the cities, leaving old Australia to ring the outer suburbs and the bush beyond. The republicans of Melbourne covered the largest area, running to all points north, east, and west of the city and as far south as Springvale Road — the barrier between the middle suburbs and the depressed areas of Frankston and Dandenong. The boundaries of Sydney republicans were west and south of the harbour — the battler line of Penrith, Parramatta, and Bankstown to the left of the city centre, and the Georges River below it. Brisbane republicans were contained in the inner city and leafy west. Adelaide republicans could be found in the centre, south, and east. Perth republicans were anchored to the west of the city, in exclusive beachside suburbs. Canberrans were a republic all over. The Northern Territory would have been a republic if an extra 1124 voters had ticked 'yes' instead of 'no'.

This wasn't merely a tale of higher incomes and higher qualifications making electorates more likely to support the republic on offer. The most common factor among the 'yes' electorates was their ethnic colouring. Overall, only 42 seats voted 'yes' for the republic — less than one in three of the nation's 150 electorates. But thirty-six of the 42 were electorates with overseas-born populations above the national average.

The twist is that the 'yes' zone is not, strictly speaking, new Australia as the media thumbnails it. Nor is it both parts of our Generation W. There is a gender gap on the republic that is often overlooked. The July 2001 Newspoll reaffirmed that majority support for a republic came from men — 56 per cent in favour,

31 per cent against. Women remained to be convinced, with 48 per cent for and 39 per cent against. In November 2002, men became even more pro-republic (57 per cent for, 29 per cent against), while women were slightly less so (46 per cent for, 41 per cent against). There are more than enough men in both the cities and bush who want an Australian head of state. The referendum went down to the extent that it did in 1999 because some women in new Australia and many in old Australia were put off by the old boys' club of the 'yes' campaign: Sydney merchant banker Malcolm Turnbull; Melbourne comedian Steve Vizard; and the over-caffeinated Collingwood Football Club president, game-show host, and footy commentator Eddie Maguire. The monarchists, for their part, had a woman at the head of its public campaign, Kerry Jones. Celebrity male republicans, like male politicians generally, don't impress women. The referendum was, in fact, a signpost to the 'de-blokeing' of Australia. Another clue was the debate over the word 'mateship', which was the second part of Howard's referendum.

To refresh our memories, we need to take a detour, to pay tribute to the Aussie god of plain speaking. Our icon doesn't have a name — we are too bloody egalitarian for that, mate. But you can catch a glimpse of him in most men, straight or gay, who have enjoyed fame in this nation. In popular culture, the spirit has moved from Dad and Dave, to Graham Kennedy, to Molly Meldrum. In sport, it was personified in the troika of the handlebar moustache: Ian Chappell, Dennis Lillee, and Rod Marsh. In politics, it has compelled every prime minister since Billy Hughes to use blunt language to snag votes. It is a role too good for women to play, which is why Aunty Jack and Dame Edna were and are fellas.

Howard sees himself in this great tradition of the uncomplicated Australian. His 'Future Directions' manifesto carried the subtitle: 'It's Time for Plain Thinking'. On becoming prime minister in 1996, Howard said one of the reasons voters embraced him was because they were sick of Paul Keating's political correctness. Confident that most Australians saw the world his way, Howard asked the electorate to outlaw Keating-speak at the 1999 referendum. Howard penned an introduction to the constitution that, he explained, contained 'a gentle rebuke to political correctness'. The preamble also praised 'mateship', a word that he said had a 'hallowed place in the Australian lexicon':

> It really has. And it not only talks about the bonds between men, but it also talks about the bonds between men and women, women and women and people.[3]

Nothing is ever that simple with Howard. The referendum wasn't held with the preamble in mind. The main purpose was to keep his promise for a vote on a republic, made at a more vulnerable time as opposition leader in 1995. The pro-mateship, anti-PC preamble was added as an afterthought so Howard could encourage the public to say yes to something.

The most instructive part of this episode is that Howard quickly dropped mateship from the final draft. It hadn't met with the favour he hoped for. When the preamble was eventually put to the people it went down by an even bigger margin than the republic — 39.34 per cent for, 60.66 per cent against. An extra 1,351,672 people voted against Howard's prose than they did against the turgid republican model on offer. So what was going on? Did the referendum mean we were pro-Queen and anti-mateship? Why did we pass up the opportunity to ban political correctness? Howard said that the verdict on the republic proved that 'Australians are very savvy'. But the preamble, he said, 'was probably defeated by apathy or ignorance, not hostility'.[4] Plainly, he couldn't have it both ways. The real message, almost five years later, is that we didn't embrace the mates of the 'yes' campaign or a preamble devoted to the myth of mateship because we are somewhere between a savvy and an apathetic nation. The electorate was indeed 'very savvy' on the referendum: it rejected the disunity of the republican lobby. It also had the sense to deny Howard the ego-trip of placing his version of Australia on the cover of the constitution. But republicans also allowed themselves to be hoodwinked by spoilers such as Reith, who said that 'no' would eventually mean 'yes'.

Politicians with long careers in public life are prone to attacking themselves. They do this unconsciously by making statements that confirm the cynicism of an earlier ploy. It was Howard who, in the end, exposed the rigging of the republican referendum. The concession came in August 2003, when he debated whether the constitution should be amended to curb the powers of the Senate:

> The history of referenda in this country is that unless both sides back the proposal it won't get up ... Whilst I think this [Senate reform] is a desirable reform, unless we have a real hope of getting it up, there's no point in putting it up.[5]

By this logic, Howard knew that the vote in 1999 wasn't a genuine opportunity to create a republic. After all, our plain speaker had written the question he wanted rejected. He asked whether voters approved of:

> A proposed law: *To alter the Constitution to establish the Commonwealth of Australia as a republic with the Queen and Governor-General being replaced by a President appointed by a two-thirds majority of the members of the Commonwealth Parliament.*

A bipartisan model stands a better chance in the future —

provided the prime minister of the day doesn't play a double game like Howard did. What is most compelling about the three Rs is that more than 40 per cent of the public were motivated to express support for agendas that Howard preferred not to have discussed. These arguments occurred in spite of Howard. He didn't start them, but he did win them when it counted. But who will fly the flag for the monarchy when he's gone?

* * *

The women of new Australia are a black hole for the print media business because they don't like reading the news we serve up. At the *Australian*, a proudly pro-republican newspaper, market researchers once painted a picture of its lost reader: a 30-something professional they christened 'Katherine McWilliam'. What this ad agency caricature reveals is another angle to the schism between new Australia and those who run it. The highly qualified, highish-paid woman has no interest in consuming politics, a staple of journals such as the *Australian*. She isn't only rejecting this particular broadsheet, but the very idea of what it reflects. To adapt a media truism, the person who buys the *Australian*, the *Sydney Morning Herald*, or the *Age* is a middle-aged man who either runs the country, wants to run the country, or wished he still ran the country.

Going into the 2001 election, the Howard ministry of 30 contained three women and 27 men. More than one in three of those ministers had female press advisers. At the 2001 election, all but one of the capital city newspapers were edited by baby-boomer-and-older men. The exception was Jeni Cooper at the *Sunday Daily Telegraph*, only the second woman in history to serve as editor after Michelle Grattan at the *Canberra Times* in the mid-1990s. Despite covering a male domain, the senior reporting jobs in Canberra's press gallery has a healthy mix of men and women. Parliament and the press gallery are in step with the broader community, where women rise in all but the very top jobs. When the Prime Minister's daughter, Melanie Howard, became a corporate lawyer, she joined Clayton Utz, a firm in which 72 per cent of the senior positions belonged to men. And this was one of the more feminine hierarchies in Sydney. She moved to Gilbert and Tobin, where just under 80 per cent of the partners, consultants, and special counsel were men. Yet Melanie graduated from the University of Sydney Law School, where women have outperformed men each year since 1990. Just like the children of immigrants in the 1970s and 1980s, the women of new Australia saw a law degree in the 1990s as a symbol of upward mobility.[6]

The Australian Republican Movement took the women of Generation W for granted. When it realised late in the referendum that women across the board were bored with the debate, the brauns trust decided to lift the campaign by wheeling out a man in his late sixties. Former Liberal prime minister Malcolm Fraser was chosen because he polled well amongst conservative, middle-class stay-at-home mothers. As a token to the left, Hazel Hawke, ex-wife of Bob Hawke, was also elevated.

These are symptoms of a society that, at best, doesn't understand or, at worst, tries to ignore women. When the first female judge in the High Court, Mary Gaudron, retired in February 2003, Howard appointed a man in her place. This left the custodian of the constitution with a bench of six straight men, and one gay one. Perhaps there is a cultural thesis to be written one day by a researcher who finds that the real reason women don't want to rule is that they know it's a career path for suckers. A more benign explanation may be that the boss tends to come from the previous generation. It may be another decade or so before enough baby-boomer-and-older men vacate head office. Even if this were to be the case, it doesn't resolve the current dichotomy. The worker who best represents new Australia — the professional woman — has as much chance today of seeing her views reflected in one of the main political parties or media outlets as, say, the next baby gorilla to be born at the Melbourne Zoo. She will be seen, even oohed and aahed over, but not heard.

This is not to suggest that we fire all the fellas — that risks swapping one bias for another, and one reader for another. The media, like politicians, work best when they cater for as many tastes as possible. What is important here is to acknowledge the consumer who does not have a political voice or the cash to match her credentials: the new Australian woman.

* * *

The Keating–Howard economy delivered more jobs, and more job insecurity. The Reserve Bank of Australia estimates that fewer people are retrenched, on average, from one month to the next than they were at the start of the 1980s, when the economy was still chilled out behind the tariff wall. New Australia's danger of slipping a rung or two down the income ladder comes not from retrenchment, but by having your hours cut. Today, workers are twice as likely to move from full-time to part-time work from one month to the next than they were two decades ago. This is a bigger problem for men than women, because they still hold the majority of full-time jobs.[7]

The Keating–Howard agenda has given us more choice than any generation before. But aspiration is a drug that also raises our levels of angst. Generation W just can't be satisfied. The market provides more than enough by way of material spoils, but the human condition ensures we find something else to grizzle about. We are feeling well-off yet unloved, victorious yet vulnerable. Secret polling conducted for the Australian Council of Trade Unions (ACTU) shows that many workers would prefer a pat on the back from the boss ahead of another pay rise. The study tested the views of both old and new Australia, in Sydney, Melbourne, Brisbane, the Victorian coastal-industrial town of Geelong, and the Queensland mining town of Bundaberg. Most people questioned did not belong to trade unions:

> When asked what they might change about their employment if they had the opportunity, most suggested acknowledgement — recognition that they were appreciated, that they were making a contribution. Relief from excessive workloads — at least temporarily, many accepted that heavy workloads would remain. And opportunities for advancement — younger workers.
>
> Acknowledgment and recognition of their value was probably the most important factor. Workers want to be able to enjoy their work and have their contribution recognised. 'I think happiness in your job is most important,' (said one worker). 'Just getting a pat on the back occasionally would be worth another $10–$20 a week' (said another).
>
> Almost no one suggested higher wages — you'd just be expected to do more, tax would take most of it, the employer might go broke. Many felt that asking employers to pay out more would only lead to job losses.[8]

The attitudes of old and new Australia diverged on what the loss of job security meant for their own lives. The older worker cited it as a cause for anxiety. The younger worker saw it as an opportunity: 'younger workers were less concerned — they did not expect to work in the same job for many years'. Old and new united in blaming their work for their bad relationships: 'More flexibility in having time off would improve their quality of life, especially those with families'. They also shared the urge to ignore politics: 'There was almost no awareness of government legislation affecting working conditions, entitlements, unfair dismissals. There was little interest or engagement with politics and political issues.'

Stripped of its market-research jargon, the message here is that an every-woman-and-man-for-themselves marketplace is not an end in itself. We still crave community, which is why we surprised ourselves by marching in the hundreds of thousands for reconciliation in 2000 and for peace at the start of 2003. The rallies were bigger than the issues themselves; they were a cry from many individuals to reconnect with their society. Our ambivalence towards the political class does not mean that we condone what it does. Generation W is a victim of its perceptiveness. The twenty- and thirty-somethings today lack the idealism of baby boomers at the same age, so politicians feel less intimidated by their views. Yet, even allowing for the different population sizes, baby boomers mustered fewer protesters for the Vietnam moratorium marches in the 1970s. Nor did the Sunbury rock festival compare as a cultural moment to the Big Day Out, which sells out every year, but gets precious little coverage in the mainstream media.

In the second half of 2001, independent academic research commissioned by the Howard government found that men were generally less satisfied with their jobs than women. The grumpiest workers were men in their twenties, followed by men in their forties. The happiest were women in their fifties, then women in their forties. The comparison between men and women in their twenties was stark. Men earned 19 per cent, or around $190, more a week on average. Yet they were 10 per cent more likely to be unsatisfied with their work.[9]

⁂ ⁂ ⁂

Generation W has yet to decide an election. The closest it came was 1998, when it helped Howard squeeze a mandate for the GST. That poll proved, ironically, that new Australia is still in the minority. While the government won a majority of seats, it lost the two-party preferred vote to Labor: 49.02 per cent to 50.98 per cent. Nevertheless, the main parties would give their left legs for a woman who could run for leader. Before they ultimately confirmed themselves to be unelectable politicians, Carmen Lawrence, the former Labor federal minister and Western Australian premier, and Cheryl Kernot, the Australian Democrats leader who defected to Labor, gave Howard a fright. Private polls during their respective public honeymoons showed that both women could shift conservative voters to the Labor side at a time when Howard was still grasping for legitimacy.

Lawrence was on course to become Paul Keating's deputy prime minister before she stumbled at a West Australian Liberal-inspired royal commission in mid-1995. The knives were drawn again when Kernot switched to Labor in October 1997. Howard and his ministers hit the airwaves to attack her credibility in the first few days after she announced her move. It was an ironic over-reaction because Kernot was no longer a parliamentarian at the time — she had quit her Senate post to run as a Labor candidate at the election the following year. Howard was still ignoring Pauline Hanson, but didn't want to grant Kernot the same privilege of celebrity. Then, suddenly, there was silence. Howard pulled his head in because his criticism seemed to increase Kernot's appeal. 'Man biffs woman' is not a good look, and he knew it. When Kernot did falter, and she did often from early 1998 onwards, Howard left it to the others to attack, including some on the Labor side. By this stage, the prime minister reasoned he could rise above it all.

Lawrence, Kernot — and even one-time Liberal star Bronwyn Bishop — are examples of the media's double standards. The kangaroo court of Australian public opinion condemned all three to purgatory on the charge of failing to meet expectations. All politicians should be treated this way. But the women received a much harder time than men in the same position. The difference can be seen in the talkback index, the measure of how many callers express an opinion on the issues of the day.

In 1995, radio listeners judged Lawrence as the biggest story of the year. The former Western Australian premier had sailed into federal parliament a year earlier, securing a swing to Labor in the by-election for the seat of Fremantle. But she was dogged by a state scandal. Three years earlier, a Labor MP had tabled a petition in the Western Australian parliament on behalf of Perth lawyer Penny Easton's ex-husband. It dealt with his side in their marriage bust-up, a private matter that should never have been aired in this way. It was one of the nastiest political episodes of the decade; Easton committed suicide a few days later. Lawrence claimed she had no prior knowledge that someone from her government planned the attack, under parliamentary privilege, on Easton. The scandal went national in 1995, after some of Lawrence's former colleagues contradicted her recollection of events in 1992. She didn't budge, so the Western Australian coalition government of Richard Court called in retired judge Kenneth Marks to grill her. The longer Lawrence maintained she knew nothing, the more trouble the Keating government got into. The most stunning aspect of the Lawrence saga, looking back, is the issues that were rated by radio listeners at numbers two to five. She outpolled French nuclear testing in the Pacific; the republic; the split in Rugby League; and the 'Australia Remembers' campaign to mark the fiftieth anniversary of the end of World War II.

In 1996, another woman topped the talkback survey. Hanson's anti-Aboriginal and anti-Asian immigration statements out-ranked gun control, Paul Keating, and the Howard government's social security policies. Hanson, unlike Lawrence, enjoyed twice as many positive callers — 54 per cent compared to 25 per cent. In 1997, Hanson again eclipsed the death of Princess Diana, the Howard government's native title policies, the republic, aged care, and work for the dole. Only this time, Hanson's support had fallen to 41 per cent. It wasn't until 1998, when the waterfront dispute and the GST bumped Hanson down into third place, that the radio public dropped its obsession with minority politicians: women.[10]

Kernot is a more disjointed case-study. Like Lawrence, she was also accused of being economical with the truth. Like Lawrence, she paid a heavy price in bad press. Kernot's political sin of adultery was judged by the media to be more worthy of attention than final proof that the government told a whopper during the 2001 election campaign when it said asylum-seekers threw children overboard. In July 2002, the week when Kernot's long-ended affair with former Labor foreign minister Gareth Evans was confirmed, Kernot earned mentions in 106 articles in capital-city broadsheet and tabloid newspapers. Earlier that year, when it was revealed that Reith had not passed on advice received from the acting head of the Defence Forces, Angus Houston, that boat people had not tossed their children into the ocean, the former defence minister featured in 72 reports in the same newspapers.[11] Here were two ex-politicians. Kernot had already lost her seat at the hands of voters; Reith had resigned, and was working as a lobbyist for the defence industry. One was an equal party in a private betrayal of two families; the other misled voters by not correcting the record in an ultra-emotive election contest. On any objective assessment, Kernot's folly does not compare with the false claim that the government peddled during the 2001 campaign. After Houston's advice to Reith was revealed, the now ex-minister offered the excuse that his mobile phone reception had been poor. Yet it was Kernot who was deemed to be 47 per cent more newsworthy.

It is, in part, to do with gender. The media, like the political parties, are hanging out for the first decent woman politician to help reconnect the people with their parliament. But waiting for Xena, the political warrior princess, is a self-defeating wish. Every woman who is excitedly promoted as a saviour faces an excruciating media and public slaying after she is shown to be a mere politician. Kernot never warranted the gushing coverage that followed her in her glory days. Nor did she deserve the twin double standards of seeing her part in the fling gain wider comment than Evans and, more importantly, the topic being raised in the first place. The hypothetical worth pondering is: what would have happened if the roles had been reversed and it was Kernot fibbing about asylum-seekers? Would she have scored more headlines than a former male politician caught with his pants down?

The demise of Lawrence and Kernot does not remove the pressure for change. The language of politics, and the way we reflect it in our media, suffers from a lack of genuine female perspective. The male ideal for new Australia is to wipe out the last vestiges of trade union power and to cut the top personal income tax rate. It is the war cry of politicians such as Costello, Howard's nominated but rebuffed successor as prime minister. Women would prefer co-operative workplaces that give them the chance to duck out to collect children from grandparents, crèche, or school. They want a stronger commitment to spending on health and education. Those who choose to stay at home would prefer not to be judged as behind the times. The interests of men and women do not have to be mutually exclusive. We can have both deregulation and a decent social policy. The point that economists and bleeding hearts have always agreed on is that the market doesn't know how to place a value on community.

* * *

One of the redeeming features of our political system is its conservatism: it forces Labor, traditionally the party of social change, to make itself clearly understood before it can take government. We know from public polls in mid-2003 that Labor under Simon Crean and Kim Beazley were not up to this challenge. However, the opposition's failure to offer an alternative does not mean that Howard can be considered a new-millennium man any more than the three-time Labor election loser Arthur Calwell made Robert Menzies a symbol of the swinging 1960s.

Our federal voting system has a habit of changing government with a time lag, usually one election after society has moved on. Add the inherent instability of a three-year term, and even well-meaning governments become more concerned with managing the political cycle than with generating policy innovation. Gough Whitlam was a 1960s man. But he made it to office, finally, at the end of 1972, by which time many of the social reforms he introduced were taken as a given. The greatest challenge for Australia's political class in the 1970s was to navigate the economy through the murky waters of stagflation. Rising unemployment and inflation became a reality — the twin evils that economic textbooks of the Keynesian era said was not possible. Whitlam was out of his depth on economics, and was the wrong man for this new test of public policy.

Malcolm Fraser came to power in 1975 with a mandate to fix the mess, but he proved to be a Whitlam in wolf's clothing: progressive on social policy, and a promoter of big government. He secured one election win too many in 1980, then allowed the budget to explode into deficit as unemployment and inflation achieved double digits in unison with the recession of 1982–3. The Hawke–Keating era is the exception that proves the point. The strength of this government was economics, but voters returned Labor for a fifth term in 1993 despite policy blunders that made recession more painful than it needed to be. The electorate was rewarded for its verdict with the broken promise that defined the first half of the 1990s: the L.A.W. income-tax cuts. Keating offered two rounds of tax cuts to voters in 1993, to be paid in 1994 and 1996, but vowed he would not need a GST to fund them. He placed those tax cuts into legislation ahead of the election, thus trumping similar tax cuts that the Liberals had on the table as part of their GST policy. What made the betrayal so stunning was that, immediately after the election, Keating cancelled the second half of the tax cuts, and increased indirect taxes to offset the cost of the first round. L.A.W. had turned, as the Liberals said at the time, into L.I.E.

What the elections of 1980, 1993, and 2001 have in common is that the opposition leaders of the day, Bill Hayden, John Hewson, and Kim Beazley, were not good enough to topple what were fast becoming very unpopular governments. When politicians win against the odds, as Fraser, Keating, and Howard did, they mistake victory for a vindication of their personal values. Howard, for all his late-career popularity, is still a politician who wants to prevent a republic, and whose prime handout to families at the 2001 election assumed women still had five years to spare to raise children. Australians have often elected governments greyer than themselves. What is unusual about the situation today is that most politicians, both Liberal and Labor, have no practical experience of working in the economy for which they are setting the rules of engagement. Politics is one of the final frontiers of protection. The rift between parliament and the people cannot be repaired whilst politics remains a closed shop for baby-boomer-and-older men.

IT'S THE LAND OF THE FAIR GO AND THE BLACK STAY HERE...

CHAPTER SIX

Unfinished Business: reconciliation

> 'I don't know any Aboriginal millionaires. If you find one, can you give me their name?'
> —Thirty-something tertiary-educated Australian Aboriginal woman living in inner Sydney, September 2002

THERE ARE ALMOST TWICE AS MANY Australian Aboriginal men in prison as there are at universities or other tertiary institutions. Count them: 4075 incarcerated versus 2482 on campus. Fortunately, Australian Aboriginal women do not repeat this bleak trend. There are only 370 behind bars against 4646 with their noses in books, a ratio of 1 to 12 to the good. So black is no different to white where male and female education is concerned. But this is where the similarity ends. Non-indigenous men have one person in prison for every 20 in higher education. Non-indigenous women have one in 35, which is almost three times ahead of Australian Aboriginal women.

It is easy to become morose about the economic, educative, and detention chasms between black and white in Australia, and easier still to switch off and pretend the problems don't exist. So let's try a different numbers game. Let's look at where economic equality seems to be in sight, the 30 per cent of Australian Aboriginals who live in the cities. This is where a young, black middle class is emerging. The place to look on the income ladder is $600–$999 a week ($31,200–$51,948 a year), the marker for the average non-indigenous earner. In August 2001, one in eight, or 14 per cent, of the 76,000 working-age urban Australian Aboriginals could be found here. The proportion of non-indigenous city slickers on the same income was one in five, or 20 per cent. The difference here is small enough to crow about. One rung below on $400–$599 a week ($20,800 to $31,148), it's line ball, with 15 per cent of blacks and 16 per cent of whites in the city in this battler band respectively. However, numbers diverge at the bottom and top. Half of all city blacks earn $399 a week or less, compared to 41 per cent of whites. And Australian Aboriginals are almost three times less likely to be on $1000-plus (5 per cent against 13 per cent).[1]

The casting of Australian Aboriginal actress Deborah Mailman as Kelly Lewis, everyone's friend in the television series 'The Secret Life of Us', almost got it right. The characters she hangs out with fit neatly into new Australia: inner-city dwelling twenty- and thirty-somethings with decent incomes but without the suburban mortgages and marriage certificates of the Cold War middle class before them. However, unlike Kelly, the black middle class isn't flitting from dead-end job to dead-end job. They are in the professional or political class, working as lawyers or public servants.

John Howard says that Aboriginals living in the cities have already been accepted as part of mainstream western society:

> There are plenty of indigenous Australians who are fully integrated. But there are still quite a lot who aren't ... We still sort of have this physical separation, that is part of the problem. It is interesting that one of the accepted cornerstones of our immigration policy has always been that you shouldn't allow ghettoes or enclaves to develop, yet in a way — you never call them ghettoes or enclaves because they are Aboriginal

> communities — but in a way that is exactly what has happened and it is one of the difficulties we have.[2]

The notion that blacks are better off in the big smoke could be seen as a subtle way of absolving non-indigenous Australia for the third world living conditions they endure in remote communities. If integration is achievable in the city, the implication for those Aboriginals who don't make the move is that they have chosen poverty over prosperity. This case is made more directly by conservative historian Keith Windschuttle. He argues that indigenous peoples in the cities are 'miles ahead' of those in remote communities. But does that mean Australian Aboriginals should be 'brought to town'? I posed this question in September 2001 to Windschuttle. He replied:

> That's right, integration with white communities, that's not assimilation, that's integration. They choose themselves what aspect of modern culture they choose to adopt, and it usually means European education, European employment, and European health standards. But like any other ethnic group, Greeks or what have you, they can retain whatever amount of their formal culture they wanted to. The idea of retaining a traditional economy in traditional areas has been proven for 30 years to be a disaster.[3]

Windschuttle clarified that he wasn't implying forced relocation. Pause for a moment to consider the conflicting strands in our people-movement debate between black, white, and immigrant. The right says that our original Australians should be encouraged to leave the bush for the city. Yet the right says that farmers should be given subsidies to stay in the bush, on the grounds that society would be impoverished without their uneconomic businesses. The left, for its part, also wants immigrants to go to the bush, but can't seem to find a unified position on whether Australian Aboriginals should remain in remote communities. New South Wales Labor Premier Bob Carr would like to see new Australians side-step Sydney and settle in the rest of NSW where there is less cash for them to make. Of the three groups, only the Australian Aboriginal is deemed unworthy of a generous taxpayer-handout to remain in the bush if he or she chooses. Indigenous leaders such as Noel Pearson would prefer that remote communities were taken off welfare to help get them off the grog and restore self-respect; but the right only hears the first part of this message, not the second, which is that Australian Aboriginals should be entitled to live where they want to.

Given the double standards of the right and left on bush assistance, it is ironic that the income distribution of the urban black resembles that of the small-town white living in a settlement of 200 to 999 people, based on what the census told us in August 2001. The thesis that Australian Aboriginals are better off in the city holds true only when the comparison is made between Australian Aboriginals living outside the city. The income profile of the urban black resembles that of a crouched camel: a large backside pointing north (50 per cent of people on less than $399 a week) and its head poised just above ground level (5 per cent on $1000-plus a week). At least we can see its face in the city. In all other areas of the nation, the income profile looks like that of an ostrich with its head buried. In large towns, 59 per cent of Australian Aboriginals are at the bottom and 3 per cent at the top; in small towns, the sums are 74 per cent and 1 per cent; and in the bush, 65 per cent and 2 per cent.[4] However, cross-matching indigenous peoples between locations in this way is misleading. The city white also earns much more than the town and bush white. The real test isn't city Australian Aboriginals against town or bush Australian Aboriginals. It's like with like, person with person, city black with city white.

On income, our indigenous peoples are the city's second-class citizens, with too many at the bottom end and too few at the top end of town. Yet even this observation may be too generous. The tables need to be taken with two grains of salt. Black Australia was only added to the census in 1971. This has posed a headache for academics. With every national census that followed, the total population declaring themselves as Aboriginal or Torres Strait Islander Australians increased faster than the birth rate. People who had been raised white are redefining themselves as black.

The census is not always accurate. For example, it can inflate white poverty. Many of those who say they are on 0–$399 are self-funded retirees on part-time incomes, or are fibbing to the Australian Bureau of Statistics because they fear, unjustifiably, that the Australian Taxation Office is allowed to peek at the data. They can't be considered as members of the struggler class. This caveat applies less so to Australian Aboriginals because, for them, the category 0–$399 is more likely to suggest welfare than hidden wealth. There is a reasonable danger, then, that city blacks are still a generation behind their white neighbours.

The smoking gun is the age of the urban Australian Aboriginal. Most are young — 60 per cent are aged up to 24 years — and only 3 per cent live to 65 and beyond. This is a near-perfect mirror of the income tables. City whites, as we know, are a greying lot. They make babies later and, thus, have fewer of them. Almost five times as many are aged 65-plus (14 per cent). The most disturbing indicator of the crisis in remote communities is that life-expectancy is falling. Australian Aboriginals are the only citizens in the developed world to be dying younger, on average, while all others enjoy longer lives. Australian Aboriginal men have a life-expectancy of 56 years, some 21 years less than all non-indigenous men. Black women are not much better off, on 63 years, which is nineteen years below non-indigenous women generally. The life-expectancy deficits for Maoris and Native Americans are mild by comparison, ranging between five and eight years.[5]

When the right says that Australian Aboriginals have a better chance in the cities, they should mean not just a higher income but longer life-expectancy. But this is not the case. The excessive youth of the urban black is a warning that Australian Aboriginals are dying before their time in the cities as well. Immigrants tend to have higher home-ownership rates (as well as longer life-expectancy) than Australian-born folk. Yet Australian Aboriginals don't have any obvious way into inner-city property markets because their parents, if they were still alive, would most likely have been too impoverished to assist with the deposit.

Another crack in the city-equals-black-progress mantra is education. Barely half the urban Australian Aboriginals aged 15–19 years are still at school: 51 per cent of boys and 55 per cent of girls. The retention rate for white youth in the cities is 73 per cent and 77 per cent respectively. So the next generation of city blacks will be substantially less qualified than the whites. Also, they are only marginally ahead of those in large towns, where 46 per cent of Australian Aboriginal boys and 50 per cent of girls stay on after year ten. Finally, almost one in three, 31 per cent, of urban Australian Aboriginal families are single-parent households — almost double the rate for white city families (16 per cent).

* * *

Imagine if Lebanese–Australians had filled out a census form along the lines that the city blacks did in August 2001? It would be seen, correctly, as proof of an immigrant underclass, a group that had failed, for whatever reason, to become a part of the new

Australian dream. The tabloids and talkbacks would not need the Mixmaster for this one; this shock-horror story would tell itself. But the Australian Aboriginals' disadvantage does not seem to rate as news. It is as if sections of the media believed Pauline Hanson when she said that the reverse is true, that black Australia gets too many handouts.

The challenge for the adviser class is to figure out why Australian Aboriginals have never really got beyond the first phase of wogdom in more than 200 years, when it took the Greeks, Italians, Chinese, and Vietnamese a brisk 20 years to get to third and home base. Immigration has been a buzz topic since the 1980s when Geoffrey Blainey cracked the consensus of multiculturalism by criticising the pace of Asian immigration. Howard concurred in 1988, then retreated, before Hanson reheated this divisive sentiment in 1996. Demographers share the myopia of the baby-boomer feminist; they argue from the vantage point of an old Australian middle class that refuses to see the true outcast. The pages of serious research devoted to Australian Aboriginals, like the single parent, is inverse to the size of the problem.

Australian Aboriginals live apart from the Australia of the white-, olive-, and yellow-skinned, even in the cities. But that seems to be the excuse to overlook them. The public argues, instead, about the past in the same way that the Greeks and Italians who stayed in their villages after World War II debated ancient Athens and Rome: as an opiate to dull the pain of the present. The point when a relationship appears irredeemable is when one quarrels over what was said or done years ago. The bizarre beauty in this sort of stoush is that neither party needs to back down. Reconciliation has been reduced to a word game, in part because the raw numbers are too painful to contemplate. Politicians and activists argue about minutiae, such as whether sufficient numbers of Australian Aboriginal children were taken from their parents in the past to warrant being called the 'stolen generation'. The Howard government thought that only 10–30 per cent of Australian Aboriginals were affected by the practice, which did not entitle them to use the word 'generation'. In a society where every minor marketing trend is a generation, it was a strange position to take. More intriguing was the idea that one section of the community could tell another how it could and could not describe itself.

In April 2000, when debate on the stolen generation blew up, Howard confirmed, unwittingly, that voters were more sympathetic to Australian Aboriginals than the government. Initially, he defended the government document that argued 'there was never a "generation of stolen children"' against opposition claims that the phrase had been framed to divide the community: 'The document was plainly not inspired for political wedge purposes, otherwise it would not have been drafted in the indigenous branch office.'[6]

It was a slip of the tongue, of course. He was merely trying to say that there was no deliberate strategy behind the line being run by the then Aboriginal affairs minister John Herron, rather than admitting there was a desk in the PM's office devoted to the grubby practice of wedge politics.

The term 'stolen generation' resonated in the electorate, and at this point Howard appeared eager to squash it before it hurt his government. Yet this would be an argument he could not win. Just two days after defending his position with his angry aside on wedge politics, Howard returned to parliament to offer a formal apology to the stolen generation. Only it wasn't for their past treatment, but for their hurt caused by the debate on whether there had, in fact, been a stolen generation:

> Let me say, very directly to anybody in the Australian community who was in any way offended by that document, I

> am sorry about that because the document was not designed to offend anybody.
>
> I regard the reaction of some people to the submission as having been understandable. I include in that, people who either were removed themselves or had parents who were forcibly removed under past practices ... The truth is that there were many people forcibly removed when they should not have been. Nobody is pretending to deny that.[7]

Later that month, when he addressed the Anzac Day dawn service in Gallipoli, Howard was more liberal with his use of the word 'generation': 'Dusk has fallen on that great-hearted generation of Australians who fought here.'[8]

Barely 1 per cent of the Australian population (60,000 out of almost 5 million) fought at Gallipoli in 1915. They accounted for 20 per cent of the 300,000 Australians who enlisted for service in World War I. The government had already conceded that 10–30 per cent of Australian Aboriginals were affected, so it was hard to see what Howard was really worried about.

* * *

The Australian politician system, white and black, has managed to turn reconciliation into a blood sport. A sense of shrillness exists that cannot be found in any other debate between Australian citizens, with the possible exception of those who argue about motherhood stereotypes. In this environment, a prime minister in full combat-mode risks hardening community attitudes against Australian Aboriginals.

In his four decades in politics, Howard has developed an almost surreal balance between principles and pragmatism. His CV is crammed with compromises, often at a split second to midnight, and after a million words to the contrary when he vowed not to give in. The most pertinent example is the Goods and Services Tax, the accounting change that he repeatedly risked his career for. In 1996, he said a GST would 'never ever' be coalition policy again. In 1998, with a parliamentary majority big enough to gamble with, he reneged and gave the nation its second GST election of the decade. When it became clear in May 1999 that he didn't have the Senate numbers for the tax package he had taken to the ballot box in 1998, he bellowed: 'No, no, no, we are not going to exempt food'.[9] Barely two weeks later, he did.

Howard believes he knows when to play follow-the-voter and when to lead. His refusal to apologise directly to Australian Aboriginals for the past sins of white settlement, which he says 'nobody is pretending to deny', poses a simple question: which Howard is speaking? The conviction politician, arguing the case against change? Or the one taking his instructions from voters? The answer is, as it turns out, a bit of both. Australian Aboriginals are often closer to asylum-seekers in the minds of the typical voter; someone else's problem, a topic many prefer not to think about. Unfortunately, there are not enough Australian Aboriginals doing well on white terms to convince people that they are no different to them.

Opinion polls confirm majority support for Howard's brand of no-fault reconciliation that says no formal apology is necessary. But does this tell us that the electorate is prejudiced? Not quite. Most Australians would not encounter Aboriginals in their daily lives. What they see are TV images of abject poverty, athletic prowess, and Aboriginal politics. All are atypical of the non-indigenous experience; and, apart from Cathy Freeman and Patrick Johnson, or the many Aussie Rules and Rugby League stars, they are not people the electorate can relate to.

The Aboriginal and Torres Strait Islander Commission (ATSIC), the body set up as a quasi-black parliament, became the most dysfunctional organisation in the nation between 2001 and 2003. As debate edged towards confronting domestic violence in Australian Aboriginal communities, the chairman of ATSIC, Geoff Clark, was accused of rape. Clark did not see the contradiction in refusing to stand aside from his post pending the outcome of the civil case against him. A white politician in the same predicament would have had no choice. Clark was only pushed aside some two years after the rape allegations were first canvassed in the *Age* and *Sydney Morning Herald*. Even then, it was a painful and difficult political exercise. Following a series of revelations in the *Australian* of questionable travel expense claims, the Howard government suspended Clark on the pretext that he had been convicted, earlier in 2003, on charges arising from a pub brawl. The deputy chairman of ATSIC, Sugar 'Ray' Robinson, a previously convicted rapist, only resigned from his job after a second set of charges relating to his financial dealings were brought against him in mid-2003. The public has now learned to have an understandable scepticism of Australian Aboriginal politics.

Even so, it takes an act of selfishness on the part of first world Australia to ignore the third world in our midst. Australia remains a nation with a split personality on race: cosmopolitan at its core, but ambivalent about its original citizens. The politician who unwittingly confirmed this mix was Hanson. In her maiden speech to parliament in 1996, she aimed both barrels at Australian Aboriginals:

> Present governments are encouraging separatism in Australia by providing opportunities, land, moneys, and facilities available only to Aborigines ... I am fed up with being told 'This is our land'. Well, where the hell do I go? I was born here and so were my parents and children.

This passage is well known. What was overlooked at the time was that Hanson wanted immigrants to know she was on their side; she wished only to slam the door on the next intake, before we became 'swamped by Asians':

> I must stress at this stage that I do not consider those people from ethnic backgrounds currently living in Australia anything but first-class citizens, provided of course that they give this country their full, undivided loyalty.

Hanson was prepared to pass the immigrants already here, but flunk our original inhabitants. Which might explain a quirk in the membership list of Hanson's One Nation Party when it was leaked in mid-1998. Alongside the Anglo and Celtic surnames ran a large portion from northern and southern Europe.[10]

* * *

When the majority of the public shows little active concern for a minority, the nation can go one of two ways. Either a leader accepts this, or he or she tries to change the way voters think. Howard, to his credit, wants reconciliation. He probably wishes he had said 'sorry' before the debate became too personal. Consider the assessment of one senior member of the Howard cabinet at the end of 2000:

> The PM is not going to change. If he changed at the moment, he'd have the people who want an apology saying he's not sincere, and the people who didn't want an apology think he's weak, which is the majority. And he'd have everybody hate him. I suspect in hindsight, if he had his time again, he'd probably play it differently, but no one gets their time again.[11]

There was a strong view in the government that Howard regretted the way he had handled reconciliation. In fact, Howard has said as much himself:

> Nobody denies that people were taken, nobody denies that there were practices engaged in the past that by today's standards would be quite unacceptable, and we feel sorry about people who suffer the injustices and we regret them.[12]

These comments placed Howard in a unique contortion. As a private citizen, he was willing to say sorry; but, as prime minister, he deemed this to be too radical a position for his government. As he showed with Asian immigration in the late 1980s, Howard is reluctant to lead his conservative supporter-base on social issues when they touch the raw nerve of national identity. He is also prepared to use hyperbole to mount the defence; a character trait that ensures the debate becomes increasingly personal. The then opposition leader, Kim Beazley, should have seized the opportunity of Howard's private 'sorry' by saying, 'Labor accepts your apology, now let's move on to practical reconciliation'. Howard was hardly going to say in reply: 'No, I didn't mean it'. But it was easier for the government and opposition to pretend that their positions on the stolen generation were too incompatible to debate. The future of Aboriginal Australia, like immigration, is a subject that demands bipartisanship; or, if there is disagreement, a discussion without rancour. When this doesn't happen, some of our most vulnerable Australians can be made to feel unwelcome in their own country.

Howard was all over the place on reconciliation in 2000, a problem that didn't repeat itself in 2001 and 2002 because tax, *Tampa*, and terror, in that order, proved to be easier topics for him to manage. But it's worth taking one final look at 2000 to see what it shows us about community attitudes. Howard discouraged Peter Costello from joining the 28 May reconciliation walk across Sydney Harbour Bridge. However, he did allow other Liberal ministers to participate. This flexible position can be explained by politics. The sanctioned walkers all held northern Sydney electorates, the pro-republic seats that Howard felt he could not afford to offend. Howard stayed in Canberra that Sunday where, perhaps fittingly, it snowed.

The following day, the Prime Minister was again on the defensive:

> I'm sorry that a lot of people don't agree with me on that, but I can't say something I don't believe. It's just no good a prime minister, no matter what criticism he cops, saying something he doesn't believe.[13]

It was a nonsense argument, of course, because he was sorry as a private citizen. Yet by the time the Olympics came and went, Howard had become more confident of his political position. In October, Newspoll showed most voters didn't want an apology:

> I thought the Newspoll was very interesting. It said what I think everybody feels, that the Olympic games were good for reconciliation. But it also makes the point that the majority of people still oppose a formal apology. The message is that reconciliation does not equal a formal apology.[14]

Even after Cathy Freeman's gold medal, voters were not sufficiently troubled by the plight of Aboriginal Australia to demand that Howard pay lip service with the s-word.

If Howard had led the debate by pushing for an apology, a majority would have quickly formed behind him. As he found on the GST, an opinion poll on any given day counts for nought if a leader is prepared to argue the case for change. Genuine contrition from the government would have shifted the onus back onto Australian Aboriginal politicians. Imagine an apology delivered at the same time as ATSIC was abolished and replaced with a more focused and accountable body? Yet Howard remains, on one level, out of step with public opinion and even with his own party. He finished the year 2000 with a speech that declared reconciliation an 'unstoppable force':

> Indigenous Australians have suffered enormously in the past and, as a defined group, continue to do so. No one can, nor should attempt to deny the devastating impact the introduction of western culture has had upon their civilisation.[15]

This speech wasn't too far off the sentiment Paul Keating had expressed in his Redfern speech eight years earlier:

> The starting point must be to recognise that the problem starts with us non-Aboriginal Australians. It begins, I think, with that act of recognition. Recognition that it was we who did the dispossessing. We took the traditional lands and smashed the traditional way of life. We brought the diseases. The alcohol. We committed the murders. We took the children from their mothers.[16]

Of course, there are details that Howard disagrees with. But here's a radical thought to chew over: Howard is closer to Keating on this issue than are many of his own colleagues. At the 2001 election, the candidates of the main and minor parties were polled for their personal views on various issues. Run by the Australian National University's research school of social science, this is a unique and widely respected opinion poll in political circles. It tests the attitudes of political candidates across the spectrum. On reconciliation, the question that sticks out is, 'Government help for Aborigines'. Almost half, 41.6 per cent, of coalition candidates surveyed, said that the government had 'gone too far' or 'gone much too far'. Another 46.4 per cent said the government had got it 'about right', while 11.5 per cent answered 'not gone far enough' or 'not gone nearly far enough'.[17]

The quirkiest part of this story, though, is that the term 'practical reconciliation', which the coalition used to differentiate its product, is not a Howard original. Guess who said the following:

> There has been no shortage of guilt, but it has not produced the responses we need. Guilt is not a very constructive emotion ...Perhaps when we recognise what we have in common we will see the things which must be done — the practical things.

That was Keating, from his Redfern treatise. The true failure of leadership is not Howard's alone. The opposition also bears responsibility for the stalemate. Before the *Tampa* sideswiped Labor in 2001, Kim Beazley was happy to play word games with Howard on reconciliation because he thought it would win him votes. All it did was to keep the nation divided on an issue where bipartisanship is a precondition for progress.

* * *

Ancient history can be a place worth investigating. Historian Keith Windschuttle has been involved in a hot-tempered debate which questions whether white settlers murdered as many Australian Aboriginals in the past as had been claimed by a number of academics. The aim of this conservative reassessment is to lift one of the veils of victimhood from Australian

Aboriginals. So let's engage in this debate by challenging another myth, held by both right and left: that of the Aboriginal as a primitive nomad before white contact. Perhaps if we can see Aboriginals as people, not as historic artefacts, we can get closer to knowing one another. This, as all sides agree, should be the ultimate goal of reconciliation. The following is a feature article I wrote for the *Australian* in August 2002:

> There is a cluster of fire-scarred eucalyptus trees in western Victoria that should help change the way people — white and black, right and left — think about the meaning of the word 'Aboriginal'. A hearth-shaped cavity is burned into the bottom of each trunk. In some, this hole has punched through to the other side, so the trees seem to be standing on thick stilts. They look like primitive ovens. The local Gunditjmara people called them 'cooking trees'. Their existence is not news to the Australian Aboriginal community or to some of the scientists who have been arguing about the ancient stone huts and fish traps found around Lake Condah, about 350 km west of Melbourne.
>
> But the combination of the trees, the huts and the traps is set to reignite the debate on whether all Australian Aboriginals were nomads before the Europeans arrived — the broad brush of the noble savage that still touches 2.2 per cent of the nation's population. Archaeologist Heather Builth, of Adelaide's Flinders University, says she has new evidence that the trees were used for smoking eels. Crucial to this theory is her discovery of traces of eel oil at the base of the hollowed trees. She believes the trees were the stove and the pantry that went with the house; the technology that could support a settled community. Builth estimates that up to 600 people might have stayed in the area.
>
> She says she thinks the traps are more sophisticated than

previously thought and were part of a water diversion structure covering about 30 km. The eels were kept in dams until maturity, then fished out, smoked and stored beside the small stone and thatched huts that served as shelter.

Builth presented her research to an international archaeological conference at the University of Durham, in northern England, later that month. 'They had the means to be sedentary,' she says, using the understated jargon of her profession. Her thesis has been backed by Flinders University associate professor Donald Pate, who is also editor-in-chief of the Australian Archaeological Association's journal, *Australian Archaeology*. It has also received encouragement from anthropologist Ron Brunton, a leading sceptic in indigenous affairs who has advised mining companies facing native title claims. 'It seems very plausible that in certain well-favoured areas you've got something akin to semi-permanent settlement,' Brunton says. 'I don't think you're in any real danger of being suddenly shot out of the water and [told]: "Look, you have been fed a real fraud here".'

Builth's paper is expected to attract praise and criticism. More importantly, it should presage a wider debate, one that University of Queensland associate professor Ian Lilley believes Australia has to have. 'It's going to have implications for blackfellas as well as for whitefellas', Lilley says. One interested observer is Tim Fischer, the former deputy prime minister who courted controversy in 1993 by saying Australian Aboriginals had not developed substantial buildings, roadways or even a wheeled cart. Fischer says he regrets that statement because he was wrongly interpreted as arguing that ancient Australian Aboriginals lacked sophistication. 'Clearly substantial new findings must always be taken into account in updating the profile and image of the previous civilisations — I use the plural deliberately — of this great country', Fischer says. 'I am the first to learn more about this and adjust accordingly.'

Lake Condah has also caught the attention of environment minister David Kemp, who is thinking about nominating the area for world heritage listing. Kemp has visited the site, which he believes has strong environmental as well as archaeological importance. Lindsay Saunders finds an obvious source of bragging rights in the idea that he is a direct descendant of the nation's first irrigators, a people who developed kilometres of canals and dams to harvest eels on their way to what is now the Great Ocean Road and who used the cooking trees to preserve them for later eating. 'We didn't have houses like this', Saunders says, pointing to the buildings at the Lake Condah Mission, the community centre from where he runs a tourist business. 'We had stone huts. We were living in a civilised manner of our own, we had villages where there were hundreds. We weren't nomads, we did stay in the one spot.'

So how did the study of Australian Aboriginal life 4000 to 8000 years ago become sexy enough to influence conservative politicians such as Fischer and Kemp? Lilley, an executive of the World Archaeological Congress, says Australians grew up with the false image that all Australian Aboriginals were the same and had not evolved since the Stone Age. 'You had two kinds of views: the romantic noble savage and the brutal savage,' he says.

The noble savage was idealised by the left as a superior socialist being, at one with the environment, anti-hierarchical, and anti-materialistic. The brutal savage, in contrast, needed a dose of modernity.

Both sides were wrong, Lilley says. In fact, a city-country divide existed before white settlement — most Australian Aboriginals who lived near the coast were relatively more advanced than those who lived inland. 'Because everyone around the coast got killed off or assimilated very early, the idea of what Aborigines were for a very long time was what was in the desert,' Lilley says. 'What we have got at the moment is this idea that yes, there was change. They remained hunter gatherers, they didn't turn into agriculturalists, but they were less like the desert stereotypes.'

The true nomad, then, might be the federal politician, who commutes from his or her electorate to Canberra and all points in between where there is a free meal to be had.

Archaeology is comparatively new in Australia, beginning as a discipline only in the 1960s. It is still a long way from consensus on the nature of these complex hunter-gatherers, the postmodern definition of the ancient Australian Aboriginal. Lilley had not seen Builth's results at the time I interviewed him and urged caution. 'The huts are a matter of debate ... some of them may well have been [huts] but not all of them that have been claimed as huts are huts. The same with trees; you have got to be very, very sure.' But he says if Builth could demonstrate that the cooking trees were used to smoke eel, then she will have broken new ground. 'The general view that she is taking is well accepted in the scientific community but, as always, the devil is in the detail. Even if she can't prove all of it, at least some of it takes us further down the track.'

Pate passed Builth's PhD with few amendments. 'I think Heather's work is probably providing more evidence of archaeological sedentism,' Pate says. Builth called in Australian National University's visiting fellow Barry Fankhauser to check the cooking trees. His tests supported her hunch. Builth also used a computer to simulate river flow before white settlers drained the swamp. This digital map shows a more involved system of aquaculture — harvesting fish — than has been argued by other archaeologists.

The caricature of the noble savage has played a corrosive

role in the reconciliation impasse between the Howard government and Australian Aboriginal groups. Reconciliation minister Philip Ruddock earned the wrath of the black and white left in 2000 when he explained to two foreign newspapers why Australian Aboriginal communities remained disadvantaged. 'We're dealing with an indigenous population that had little contact with the rest of the world. They didn't have chariots. I don't think they invented the wheel,' Ruddock told the *Washington Post* in July 2000. Hal Wootten, one the royal commissioners into Australian Aboriginal deaths in custody, replied that when faced with European settlement, the indigenous peoples did not have trouble with the wheel but the values of white society.

Builth believes the smoked eels may have been used as currency and that the community at Lake Condah involved at least two classes of people. She thinks these Australian Aboriginals were closer to the Native Americans, who had chiefs. A potential hot spot in this debate will be whether the notion of the complex hunter-gatherer affects how some Australian Aboriginals see themselves politically today. Lilley, who is a reader at the University of Queensland's Aboriginal and Torres Strait Islander unit, says there is a paradox that must be confronted. 'As archaeology is saying to the community: "Check this out, we have got all this diversity through time", Aborigines, for political reasons and just because they were educated in this way, have said: "No, we have unchanging people in an unchanging culture". But this timelessness thing has painted them into a corner, in terms of native title, for instance. If you look at the way the court defines tradition and all those sorts of things, it's very much this timelessness thing.'

This is why the discovery of a more complex past may be necessary to help remove some of the complexity in the present dialogue and allow Australian Aboriginals to move on.[18]

I'M NOT A RACIST BUT I MIGHT BE SHORTLY....
INTERNAL POLLING

CHAPTER SEVEN

Howard's Way

> 'My claim is not that he is a racist; I don't believe that at all. It's just that he couldn't resist the temptation, the opportunism, of saying, when he thought it was palatable, that we should cut the [Asian immigration intake].'
> —Paul Keating, radio interview, February 1995, two weeks after John Howard's resurrection as opposition leader

JOHN HOWARD USES LANGUAGE in the same way that Bob Hawke did as prime minister. He is imprecise, yet creates the impression of certainty. It is an asset in the age of sameness, where the visual and the vocal matter more than the printed word. Yet their bet-each-way speech patterns can also be a weakness. Neither is worth reading at length; their transcripts often leave you numb. The quotes they are remembered for are the unscripted ones, when they were too direct for their own good: Howard's 'never ever' GST; Hawke's 'no child shall live in poverty' gaffe at his July 1987 election campaign launch. There is something else that Howard and Hawke have in common. Both played the refugee card at a federal election. Howard's war on boat people in 2001 was not a new idea; Hawke ran a similar line against Vietnamese asylum-seekers in 1977, when Howard was Malcolm Fraser's treasurer.

Before we look at what Howard's refugee election reveals

about us as a nation, as reflected in the private polling of the main political parties, we need to get to know Howard a little better. The place to start is where his friends and foes least expect it: 1984.

The scene is a typical day of debacle for the then Liberal opposition. Andrew Peacock is leader; Howard, his stalking deputy. Historian Geoffrey Blainey has delivered his prophecy that the Hawke government's immigration policies would lead to the 'Asianisation of Australia'. His comments give the Liberals heartburn. Some MPs are tempted to end four decades of bipartisanship between government and opposition on the issue of race. Until this point, it has been an article of faith on both sides that the national interest of a large immigration program outweighed any short-term political gain to be made by exploiting the electorate's fear of new arrivals. If you asked political junkies today who was the Liberal politician who first tested public opinion on how many more immigrants we should accept, the answer would probably be Howard. The opposite is true. It was Peacock who took Blainey's bait in 1984. Howard, as fate would have it, thought his rival made a mistake.

In May 1984, Peacock unhinged his party by suggesting that the rate of Asian immigration needed to be lowered to preserve the 'European nature' of the program — not by reducing the intake, but by re-booting the European component. It wasn't a plausible policy because the Mediterranean was already drying up as a source of working-age immigrants. The Europe of the 1980s was light years away from the aftermath of World War II. Continental citizens had less incentive to travel halfway around the globe to start a new life. Peacock quickly retreated when he realised that the debate was getting nasty, and that neither his party nor the public were sufficiently behind him.[1]

So what did the Sydney-born Howard think of this fumbled Asian immigration card from the Melbourne-born Peacock?

Howard was aghast. He confirmed this in a remarkable speech to parliament in August 1984. Howard criticised Peacock, albeit indirectly, by rebuking Hawke. His stance then is fascinating in light of what happened in 2001. Howard reminded parliament that Hawke had played the refugee card as ACTU president seven years earlier, when the Fraser government accepted Vietnamese boat people ahead of public opinion. Howard began by quoting Hawke, who said in 1977:

> Of course, we should have compassion, but people who are coming in this way are not the only people in the world who have rights to our compassion. Any sovereign nation has the right to determine how it will exercise its compassion and how it will increase its population.

Yep, you read correctly. This was Hawke demonising asylum-seekers 24 years ahead of Howard's time. Howard's brutal, off-the-cuff election slogan in 2001 — 'We decide who comes to this country and the circumstances in which they come' — had unconsciously plagiarised Hawke. If Karl Marx were alive today, perhaps he'd adjust his truism: history repeats, first as tragedy then as *Tampa*.

The Howard of 1984 accused the Hawke of 1977 of having pandered to racial prejudice in the community:

> Of course [Hawke] was then conscious that immigration and unemployment were potential issues in that election campaign and he was fairly short on liberalism and fairly strong on opportunism in the remarks that he made in 1977. He did not mind if those remarks were interpreted by Australian workers as hitting out against Asian immigration and the potential threat that that might represent to the jobs of Australians.

Howard was warming to the task of showing up the hypocrisy of Labor:

> He [Hawke] went on to say: 'Obviously there are people all around the world who have a strong case for entry into this country and successive governments have said we have an obligation, but we also have an obligation to people who are already here.' They are unexceptional remarks perhaps in another climate. But in a climate in which our government was grappling with a very difficult issue and trying to balance practicality with humanitarianism, the remarks of the then leader of the ACTU were designed to exploit a political situation, so he hoped, to the embarrassment of the then Liberal government.

Howard told Hawke that politicians had a higher duty: to 'keep race out of debate in Australia', to 'keep the temperature off the boil'. He concluded by quoting a letter he had received from 'a gentleman in Sydney with whom I attended university ... a very well-known member of the Jewish community in Sydney [who] has very high connections in the Australian Labor Party':

> He wrote a letter to me as a friend saying: 'It is very important that all of us on both sides of the political fence do everything we possibly can over the next few months to make sure that racism does not in any way intrude into the election campaign'. I agree very much with those sentiments and they were expressed in a very genuine fashion.[2]

This is by far the strongest moral rebuke for the language Howard used to prosecute his refugee policy — out of his own mouth. And the friend he cited in 1984? Marcus Einfeld, who was featured in the Sydney Boys High debate in 2002.

Something happened to the Howard of 1984. Four years later, he played his own Asian immigration card in breach of his undertaking to take the heat out of the issue — a mistake that he has long since regretted. The explanation for the backflip is simpler than the left thinks. Howard is a politician, but he has not always been a good planner. Accidents happen on his watch, often. In 1988, the roles between Howard and Peacock were reversed. Howard was opposition leader; Peacock, the disloyal deputy. Howard was a hounded man. At the time, he was considered too far to the right for the tastes of the old Liberal Party, but too timid for the liking of the new right. He grabbed the Asian immigration card when his approval rating as opposition leader was tumbling faster than the Aussie dollar during the banana-republic episode a couple of years earlier. This is not to absolve him, but to explain the context. With Howard, chaos theory is often closer to the truth than any conspiracy.

There would be further twists to this part of the made-for-television mini series. Peacock exploited Howard's Asian immigration comments as part of his campaign to regain opposition leadership in May 1989. In the corridors of parliament, the talk at the time was that the Liberals had to be rid of Howard because he 'brought race into the political debate', as one Peacock supporter put it to me. Imagine the bemusement of Howard when barely a year on, at the March 1990 election, Peacock played yet another version of the Asian immigration card. As defeat loomed in the final week of the campaign, Peacock made an issue of the multi-function polis, a joint Australian–Japanese proposal to build a high-tech city of the future. Peacock said: 'I don't like enclaves. I don't think most Australians do ... Doesn't have to be an enclave based on race. This is a very elitist concept'. Earlier in the election, Howard, who was the shadow minister, said: 'I don't think we should bury the concept in a sea of hostility before we know anything about it'.

Howard and Peacock were like two boys wrestling over the cubbyhouse rope. As one grabbed it and inched up, the other pulled at his pants. Howard was for Asians when Peacock was against them, and vice versa. The one redeeming feature of this game of musical chairs was that the bulk of the public did not want to dance with either Liberal. Having a dig at Asian immigration was not an election-winning hand for a mainstream politician in the 1980s and early 1990s. Howard has worn a chip on his shoulder since 1988. He bristled at the double standard of Peacock, and those who supported him. Howard's legendary abhorrence of political correctness had its genesis in this experience. As someone who sees himself as genuinely colour blind, the accusation that he divided the nation in 1988 cut him to the marrow. For years afterwards, he spread the blame for his Asian immigration card between 'loose language on my part' and 'fairly zealous misinterpretations by some others'. Of course, this was self-serving. But knowing what was in his head at the time makes what followed under his prime ministership a little easier to comprehend.

The audacity of the refugee card in 2001 was not so much in the intent of policy itself. Even the left concedes that Australia should not allow people smugglers to dictate the nation's immigration policy. The problem was that genuine refugees could be used as pawns in an election campaign. Reversing the burden of proof, the government ran a show trial that rejected the claims of the boat people as bogus without giving them a right of reply.

To make legal the *Tampa's* interception at gunpoint, the government required a retrospective act of parliament before the election. Later, the occupants of the 'children overboard' boat were defamed. Howard said:

> I don't want in this country people who are prepared, if those reports are true, to throw their children overboard.[3]

He never did apologise to the people on either boat, even when some were found to be 'genuine refugees'. Nor did he think it necessary to apologise to the Australian public for his government's false election-claim in the children-overboard case:

> If I, in good faith, use information and I subsequently find that some of the information was not correct, I can express a regret that that has occurred, but I haven't acted in bad faith ... If I had done something deliberately misleading, I would owe people an apology. I haven't.[4]

It was the same formula Howard employed on reconciliation: regret, not contrition. As chance would have it, the Prime Minister's wife, Janette Howard, made an interesting observation some ten days after the above quote. Mrs Howard had been moved to issue statements on consecutive days demanding an apology from Canberra press gallery journalist Glenn Milne. The offending article that Mrs Howard wanted retracted had reported the view of an unnamed cabinet minister who alleged that she, not the Prime Minister, had selected Peter Hollingworth as governor-general. Mrs Howard was furious when Milne would not back down:

> You have sought to excuse your failure to check the accuracy of the reference to me ... on the grounds that you were merely retailing what a third person had said and not yourself making the claim. With respect, this excuse is disingenuous.
>
> The rationale of your defence, apparently, is that any allegation can be contained in an article about a person, without the truth of the allegation being checked, provided the

> allegation is not of the author of the article, but merely of someone whom the author has spoken to. I find such an attitude quite unacceptable ... You owe me an apology.[5]

Meanwhile, Heather Ruddock, wife of the then immigration minister Philip, had this to say in defence of her husband after the election:

> I'm often troubled by the public perception of him [Philip]. I find it quite hurtful when you might walk through a demonstration to go to a function and you've people shouting out: 'You're a mass murderer, you're a racist'. blah, blah, blah. One thing he does not have is a racist bone in his body. Many faults he may have, but he is not a racist man.
>
> On the other hand, there are a lot of people who are supporting him in what he's doing who I feel sometimes may be supporting him for what I might see as the wrong reasons.[6]

The Howard of 1984 would have sided with Mrs Ruddock in worrying that the Howard of 2001 was giving succour to the redneck minority in the community. That the Howard of 2001 did not feel pressured to apologise for his inaccurate claims made in the children-overboard incident suggests that the electorate did not hold the matter against him. The two Howards of 1984 and 2001 can only be reconciled by the latter seeing himself as a true victim; an act of denial that only a generation's worth of PC pin pricks and daggers could have produced. This is not to discount the circumstances of 2001, when the nation was confronted by an uncomfortable proportion of asylum-seekers who said they were Afghani when they were, in fact, Pakistani. It is the language Howard employed that is the issue. On a topic where sensitivity is required, Howard used words as Exocets in defiance of political correctness. To re-quote his earlier lecture to Hawke and Peacock, 'he did not mind if those remarks were interpreted by Australian workers as hitting out against' asylum-seekers.

* * *

The puzzle with Howard is his childhood memory of immigrants, a memory that is atypically inclusive for a white Aussie boy in the 1940s and 1950s. The young Howard does not strike one as the type to tease the children of non-English-speaking immigrants. In an interview with me in April 2002, Howard related his first contact with Australia's first wave of immigration after World War II:

> I grew up in a suburb that is now very Greek. Both my wife and I. My wife grew up in Kingsford, which became a very Greek suburb, and I grew up in Earlwood, and Earlwood is on the edge of Marrickville, and the more affluent Greeks moved out of Marrickville into Earlwood, in the same way that the more affluent Italians moved out of Leichhardt into Drummoyne and Abbotsford. My first contact with non-English-speaking people would have been contact with Greeks at school. There would have been a small number of Greek boys, three or four in my class. A couple of them played in our local church cricket team, even though they weren't Methodist; they were probably Orthodox.

I asked, did these Greek kids have a hard time?

> Not that I remember, no, I don't. I'm not conscious of it, no. I mean I'm not saying they didn't, I'm not saying that we were perfect ... They seemed to mix, they were boys that were pretty sporty and knockabout.

Howard describes Earlwood Public School, where he first learned about immigration, as lower-middle class:

> Let me categorise it by saying that I left there in 1951 to go to Canterbury High and there would have been many in my 6A class, I reckon a good third to a half of the boys' fathers would have been tradesmen. Then there were a lot of boys whose fathers worked for the gas company, or insurance company, or with banks, who were white-collar workers. And there would have been three or four like my own dad who were small businessmen. I don't think there were any doctors or lawyers. There where a few Greeks and a couple of Chinese boys too. And when I went to Canterbury High in '52 to '56, [there were] still quite a number of Greeks. Then started to come across quite a few Estonians and Lithuanians and Latvians, a lot of Baltic boys from around Lakemba and Bankstown.

In 1996, he returned to Canterbury High as prime minister, for the 40-year reunion of his class of 1956:

> All the prefects were there — not bad for a Saturday night — to sort of welcome me at the gate, and the school captain had been born in Karachi, and he liked cricket.[7]

So how do we reconcile Howard the person with Howard the politician? Let's try the views of two Liberals who have sat beside him in government. One is a moderate, the faction that Howard purged in opposition during the 1980s; the other, a political rival. Our witness for the defence is a cabinet minister. Let's call him a small-c critic. He says Howard would prefer to be one step behind the community rather than ahead of it:

> On social issues, he has never been one to suck it and try. I

> think [his] kids have played a part in his becoming more comfortable with these things, and age has played a part too. If you go back to that 1988 [Asian immigration] debate, the whole concern was with what he saw as social cohesion. He was never opposed to multi-racial immigration, but he was concerned about the pace of it and if the community would accommodate it. Now he's looking back with the benefit of hindsight and sees that those fears weren't realised.

But this minister, who has prospered under Howard, has a harder time explaining the war on boat people in 2001:

> He [Howard] is comfortable with taking a reasonable share of those who are fleeing the Taliban. I think he is sympathetic to their plight, that they have got every reason to have fled. It's more an issue of being able to control the numbers coming here. You could say we weren't controlling it with the Vietnamese boat people, but because — and it would be very cruel to put it this way I suppose — but because those boats were so small and they were generally battling in them for long distances, in terms of [the Fraser government] controlling the total outcome, there were more literal obstacles than what there are now.[8]

Ouch, the rawness of *realpolitik*. When Australia was confronted with tiny boats containing a handful of people at a time, it was easy for the Fraser government to let them in. When larger, faster, but not more seaworthy boats were jammed with 400–500 people, and were part of an organised crime operation, a rational government said in effect: 'Bugger the human rights, we can't cope with the demand. Nor will we be dictated to by people smugglers'. There is an important subtext here. The increased number of boats coming to Australia in 2000 and 2001 were assisted by the indifference of Indonesian authorities, who had their own reasons for not co-operating with the Howard government: East Timor's independence.

A much harsher view of Howard comes from a capital-c critic, a leading Liberal who told me after the 2001 election: 'Howard's epitaph is already written. "He put race into the political lexicon for the first time in 50 years."'

This Liberal said that race politics is a vote-winner, but at the cost of national unity:

> If we asked voters, 'Do you want Melbourne to be the biggest Greek city outside of Greece?', they would have said no. If Fraser had bothered to take some polls about Vietnamese and Cambodians in 1976, people would have said no. But the difference on those occasions is that whoever was in government thought that it was something that Australia had to do, and whoever was in opposition, in the national interest happened to agree. Both sides believed, 'No, we are not going to play the race card'. The difference on this occasion was that John Howard was totally prepared to play the race card.[9]

Why, then, did Howard lose the Asian immigration debate in 1988? This Liberal replied that Pauline Hanson made it easier for Howard the next time around. She was the unwitting fall girl who made the Prime Minister appear reasonable by comparison.

The catch for these two Liberal politicians is that they share the misconception that the Australian electorate has always been inherently hostile to Asian immigration. There are a bundle of opinion polls taken 30 years before Hanson's speech to parliament that reveals attitudes to race can be as fickle as the Australian fashion industry. In November 1966, Australian Gallup Polls asked, 'How many Asians should be given permanent resident status in Australia each year?' The coalition government of Harold Holt had just lifted the intake to the then psychological threshold of four figures: 1000. One in four voters surveyed said they were happy with that higher number. Eighteen per cent wanted even more Asians to be allowed in. Less than one in five, 19 per cent, favoured a lower intake of 500, while 18 per cent wanted to 'admit none'. That left 20 per cent of voters with 'no idea'. The pollsters concluded:

> At least six out of 10 Australians favour some migration from Asia, and they are inclined to approve this year's increase to 1000 a year.

The 1966 opinion polls also revealed an Australia that did not want more Japanese cars on the market — six out of 10 wanted the quota either pegged at the existing level, or reduced. An even bigger majority favoured the monarchy — 65 per cent said, 'Keep ties with Britain', while 22 per cent wanted Australia to 'become a republic'. Today, a politician would spin this as proof that Australia could be both pro-monarchy and pro-Asian. Come to think of it, that's what Howard has been arguing.

If the Fraser government had polled voters a decade later in 1976 on whether to accept Vietnamese boat people, the answer would have been, 'Okay, sure.' But only if both sides of politics were arguing the 'yes' case. That's why Howard was so critical of Hawke; he wouldn't give the government bipartisanship on race. The argument in 2001 was not of the same nature. The question voters were asked to rule on was who had the tougher border-protection policy — John Howard or Kim Beazley. Unlike the issues of the republic and reconciliation, where one of the main parties offered an alternative, the third R was played, at the political level at least, as a consensus issue. Here the 40-odd per cent of voters who still supported refugees after the *Tampa* were doing so in defiance of both the coalition and Labor.

Public attitudes towards asylum-seekers hardened, in part, because politicians painted a different picture in the new millennium. Both the government and the opposition employed the term 'illegal immigrant'. I asked Howard after the 2001 election to clarify the difference between Vietnamese fleeing communism in the 1970s, whom the nation welcomed, and Afghanis and Iraqis on the run from the Taliban and Saddam Hussein in the new millennium, whom the government shunned. I learned later that this was a topic that other ministers had wanted to raise with Howard, but were too intimidated to do so. As a warm-up, I reminded Howard of his 1984 speech which, Paul Kelly wrote in the *End Of Certainty*, had made him briefly fashionable in the federal parliamentary press gallery. The Prime Minister chuckled:

> It's mostly when I became leader that I became unfashionable in the press gallery. As you know, putative leaders are always fashionable.

I read back to him that quote of Hawke's, and how he had savaged it as being 'fairly short on liberalism and fairly strong on opportunism':

> I remember using that argument. I do remember at the time when the Fraser government, when we had that boat people problem, it was quite hard ... Hawke was not, I didn't think at the time he was all that helpful. In 1984, he was posing as a sort of paragon of virtue, and I remember reminding him that he hadn't always been a paragon of virtue on those sorts of things.

We talked about how the community had accepted his government's recent increases to the regular immigration-intake. Like a seagull trying to pinch a chip off a crowded boardwalk, I followed up with: 'But when you look at border protection and refugees, there seems to be a disconnection in terms of the public's response to the two arms?' Uh-oh. Here I was sounding like a politician, when what I really wanted to know was why he thought Australians could be so Jekyll and Hyde about immigrants and asylum-seekers, and if he had played one off against the other, as some commentators had suggested. Howard took my half-formed question personally, which was a relief of sorts, because it meant he knew what I was getting at.

'Do you think the border-protection thing is the lightning rod, is that what you are suggesting?' he asked.

'No, that is just what your critics say', I said.

'It just happened that way. I mean if no more boat people come, the issue will recede from public consciousness, I hope. But people do draw a very strong distinction between people coming here legally and illegally. I can't say that too strongly.'

As it happens, Howard was proven correct on this score a year later when Newspoll found that immigration had fallen off the radar as an issue rated by voters as 'very important'. It helped that no boats had appeared on the horizon throughout 2002 and the first half of 2003.

Finally, I posed the moral question: 'What is the difference between Vietnamese boat people and people fleeing the Taliban or Saddam Hussein today?' It yielded the only tongue-tied answer Howard gave in our 70-minute chat:

> One of the relevant differences is that Australia had a particularly, had a specific, an atypical moral obligation in relation to Indo-Chinese people. We fought beside them, we'd been quite heavily involved. That was the dominant reason, it was one of the dominant reasons from my recollection. We'd actually fought and then people felt that, I mean we had spent years, rightly or wrongly, being involved in this very controversial war and most of these people were fleeing the

> regime that we had aligned ourselves with the South Vietnamese against. And we felt that we had a particular moral obligation to offer some [help], a particular moral obligation.

One could argue, as the government is trying to, that the toppling of the Afghani and Iraqi dictatorships reduces the onus on Australia to offer protection to refugees from these countries. The government has a policy of returning refugees to their homelands when the risk of political persecution is removed. There are, however, two contradictions in this approach. First, the Afghanis and Iraqis who were turned back in 2001 were fleeing tyrannies we had yet to go to war against. Second, the Europe we accepted refugees from after World War II was already rid of fascism. The difference is that Australia needed people in the 1940s and 1950s to rebuild its own economy. The Australia of today can afford to be choosy. Which is another way of saying that we have become insulated by prosperity. We could relate to the suffering of continental Europeans, even the Vietnamese, because we shared their plight. World War II reached our doorstep; the Vietnam War, our living rooms. The conflicts in Afghanistan and Iraq were commercial breaks by comparison; they were over quicker than you could say 'regime change' or 'weapons of mass destruction'.

* * *

The emotional left analysis assumes that Howard has been actively seeking a race card all his career. He is not that sinister. What he is, though, is the only mainstream politician of his generation who felt that immigration could be debated by the same kill-or-be-killed rules of hyperbole as any other issue. This is Howard's true blind spot on race: his language can be insensitive.

For a politician who prides himself on plain speaking, immigration and reconciliation are the only topics on which Howard can't get voters to agree on what he stands for. His supporters and opponents alike can recite his mantras on the GST, industrial relations, privatisation, gun laws, the sanctity of small business and family, even cricket. Not immigration or reconciliation. On these questions of national identity, Howard has always been a qualifier, not a clarifier. So much so that when he makes a statement which supports Australian Aboriginals or Asians, some on his side think he doesn't mean it. After the 2001 election, a Liberal frontbencher told me that Howard didn't really believe that Chinese–Australians and Vietnamese–Australians were the new Greeks and Italians. 'He had to say that', this member of the ministry said. The MP advised me that Asians came from a different culture, unlike Greeks and Italians, who were Christian: 'The Orthodox and the Catholic churches are not that far removed from ours'. I don't believe that this MP knows his boss well enough. Yet the anecdote confirms a core issue with Howard: when he speaks on immigration, some people take in whatever message suits their own prejudice.

Less than one in three (31.8 per cent) of Liberal and National Party candidates in 2001 thought there should be more immigrants allowed into Australia. Most (63.5 per cent) thought the numbers were 'about right'. Imagine their surprise, then, when Howard lifted the immigration intake above the psychological threshold of 100,000 after the 2001 election.[10]

* * *

The three big race episodes in Howard's career were all unnecessary in a political sense.

Episode I, 1984–1988: Howard learned that the Asian immigration card was not a vote winner.

Episode II, 1996–2000: a tale of two cards. Here, as prime minister, he considered forcing a double-dissolution election on native title in 1997–8 — the Wik card — before realising it could cost him his job. Either side of that, he did his best impersonation of the Fonz in 'Happy Days', unable to say s-s-sorry — the apology card.

Episode III, from August 2001: the refugee card.

To understand why even the last in this series — our third R — was not as dark a play as some on the left think, we need to first take a closer look at Hanson and Queensland, the state where the postmodern race debate began before it was overtaken by Sydney.

The Wik and apology cards, like the Asian immigration card before them, carried a personal edge for Howard. They were played at a time when he was engaged in a fight for political survival — not with Labor, but with his own side of politics. Hanson and her One Nation Party became to Prime Minister Howard what Peacock had been in opposition: a rival for the job of spokesperson for old Australia. Howard's critics make the mistake of seeing Hanson as a like-minded conservative. She wasn't. Initially, Howard made the error of seeing some of her voters as his people, mainstream Australians. As Prime Minister, Howard began his first term by encouraging Hanson's right to free speech. Yet, before that term was up, he attacked one of her speeches as 'inaccurate, dishonest [and] verging on the deranged in various places'.[11] After the 2001 election, with the threat of Hanson behind him, Howard said Australia 'had seen off our Le Pen', a reference to the extreme-right French politician who had just finished second in that nation's presidential race. What helped changed his response to Hanson was the politics around him.

Howard's opening decision in office in 1996 was to gut public funding to ATSIC, a controversial move at the time, but one which hindsight tells us may have been a necessary penalty. Hanson would not have entered his calculations; she was then a silent independent in a parliament where the coalition held a gargantuan majority. Howard's next major policy announcement, gun law reform, also had nothing to do with Hanson. The Port Arthur massacre occurred in April 1996, five months before Hanson lit her Molotov of prejudice in her maiden speech to parliament. But gun law reform became one of the issues that Hanson used to rally her niche of old Australia. Hanson would have remained a footnote in the story, a human headline without a popular support base, if Howard hadn't lost the plot soon after.

The year where it fell to pieces for Howard, and into place for Hanson, was 1997. The two biggest issues then were rorts and native title. Howard eventually lost seven frontbenchers for either fiddling with their taxpayer-funded expenses or for holding shares that conflicted with their public duties. Howard also got too close to the most unpopular politician of the era, ex-Labor Senator Mal Colston, who was now voting with the coalition. In April, Howard waited eight days before he referred allegations of rorting against Colston to the Australian Federal Police. The whiff of scandal so soon into his opening term plonked Howard in the position he knows best: underdog. It gave Hanson a ready-made constituency, blue-collar voters who had switched from Labor to the coalition in 1996 and were now annoyed with Howard.

Into this mix came Wik, the High Court's December 1996 judgment that native title co-existed with pastoral leases. Howard found Labor unwilling to negotiate with him to clarify the situation, just as the coalition had been when in opposition to Paul Keating after the Mabo ruling four years earlier. Howard was battling on two fronts — Labor on the left and Hanson on the right.

It was 1988 all over again. Howard's approval rating was pointing south, and an ultra-conservative politician was pointing her finger at him. At first, Howard grabbed the Wik card, warning the Senate he would call an early election if his legislation wasn't passed. He delivered one of the angriest speeches of his career to a reconciliation meeting in Melbourne in May 1997. It is, looking back, one of the biggest regrets of his prime ministership. He wanted to talk about Wik, but was at cross-purposes with the audience. As Howard's temper rose, people jeered, stood up, and turned their backs on the Prime Minister. It wasn't the words themselves — read in isolation they do not appear too incendiary. It was Howard's defiant tone. He barked and hectored as if he were answering an offensive question from the opposition in the bull-pit of parliament.

'I made a mistake', he said later. 'I got angry because people were interjecting on Wik. But I still shouldn't have reacted like that, it was a mistake.'[12]

By this stage, the coalition had been struggling with the concept of native title for five years. Its farming and mining constituency didn't want a bar of it. When the initial Mabo legislation passed through the Senate at the end of 1993, opposition leader John Hewson declared it a 'day of national shame'. Today, Hewson is an acidic critic of Howard's approach to reconciliation. Former Victorian Liberal premier Jeff Kennett warned that suburban backyards would be at risk of native title claim. He, too, has softened his views: 'I think that, like many others, I was trying to deal with something that was new, that was undefined.'[13]

In the 1990s, Australian Aboriginals were considered fair game to politicians, just as asylum-seekers were in the new millennium. Yet Howard eventually baulked at taking the Wik card all the way to the ballot box. To understand why, we need to check some previously secret opinion polling. The main parties began quietly questioning the electorate on race in the second half of the 1990s — a pragmatic response to Hansonism that they never admitted publicly. Both sides regularly took the nation's race temperature as a calculated by-product of focus-group discussions in which carefully selected members of the community were asked to volunteer their thoughts on the issues of the day. Slowly, but methodically, I compiled snippets of the research to test whether the electorate was indeed as racist as some politicians on both sides privately worried. This polling, once it began leaking to me, created it own momentum. It doesn't matter who provided the first documentation; it proved to be the lever to get the other side to talk. By the end of 2002, both Labor and Liberal were keen to put their spin on some of the confidential material I was shown. With off-the-record disclosures on both sides, I cross-referenced what they were — and were not — telling me with hard data from the August 2001 census, the Australian Electoral Commission, and the Newspoll surveys. Here's one of the pivotal documents dealing with native title, revealed for the first time.

In November 1997, the Queensland National Party premier, Rob Borbidge, tried to claim a position between Howard and Hanson on native title. State Labor opposition leader Peter Beattie panicked. He couldn't see how any of this would help him. Labor had just tested the attitudes of voters in marginal electorates, and the working class was somewhat hostile towards Aboriginals. The key section from the 1997 research says:

> Wik was not an up-front issue, but one which is festering under the surface, particularly in Townsville.
>
> In mid November, soft voters had no reason to identify Wik particularly with state politics — before Borbidge had flagged it as a possible election issue — and they shared the frustration of white voters elsewhere in Australia who want to

> see an end to it. They were particularly alienated by recent Aboriginal outbursts and threats to boycott the Olympics [then three years away].
>
> Despite their aversion to considering the issue involved, men in Townsville did admit that the Wik debate was likely to be a big issue for Queensland, given the exposure of the State's pastoralists to native title claims and its dependence on mining. They showed virtually no knowledge of the status of the Wik legislation, nor its content. Most comments were restricted to knee-jerk responses about the Aboriginals wanting more of everything.

One Townsville male was quoted to emphasise the potential for backlash against Australian Aboriginals: 'I feel that they've now got heaps more than they had and now they want *more*.'

Then the sting for Beattie: 'Borbidge is admired for standing out against advocates of native title and wanting stricter legislation than the federal government.'

This might help explain why Howard was flirting with a double-dissolution federal election on Wik. There was a view at the time that there would be votes in it for him. Queensland, along with New South Wales, were the two states that contributed most to his triumph in 1996, but that was also where One Nation polled the strongest in 1997. When the Queensland state election was held in June 1998, Queenslanders gave Howard a black eye. The National and Liberal Parties agreed to swap preferences with One Nation, hoping that this would keep them in power. But it cost them both ways: the conservative voter went to One Nation; the moderate, to Labor. The upshot was that Labor won minority government — the six seats it lost to One Nation were offset by the six it won off the coalition. The coalition, meanwhile, lost another five seats to One Nation and one to an independent. As a dry run for the federal election four months later, the message was obvious: Howard could be tipped out of power if he stuck too close to Hanson. The Wik card was quickly forgotten. Howard played his GST card instead, and won — just. But as chaos theory would have it, this result helped to bring the refugee card to the table in 2001.

I DON'T WANT TO PLAY THE RACE CARD SO I'LL GET RID OF THESE JOKERS...
THE 2001 ELECTION GAMBLE

CHAPTER EIGHT

The War on Boat People

'Flexibility is the first principle of politics.'
—Richard Nixon, 1967[1]

QUEENSLAND IS TOLERANT ONE DAY, terrified the next. In 2001, the state that spawned Pauline Hanson encapsulated the nation's dual identity: new and old. As Queenslanders approached the polling booths in February that year, John Howard was gripped with a disquieting sense of deja vu. A repeat of the 1998 debacle, when conservative voters migrated to One Nation and moderates to Labor, was in the sticky late summer's air. The coalition parties still didn't know what to do with Hanson. Rob Borbidge, now opposition leader, said that One Nation should be placed last on how-to-vote cards. Some MPs defied his edict, killing any chance the Nationals and Liberals had of toppling Peter Beattie. To complete the eerie refrain, Howard was again unpopular. Only this time, the revolt was deeper than it had been two-and-a-half years earlier.

There was unmistakable evidence from Liberal Party research that voters of all income backgrounds and political loyalties were in open rebellion over the implementation of the GST; especially the mountain of paperwork and higher petrol prices associated with it. One of Howard's closest supporters told me at the time that private polling showed lifetime Liberal voters were preparing to switch sides. 'When your base collapses, then you are talking landslide', he said. Kim Beazley was starting to look like the prime minister in waiting. It was into this stew, in the final week of the state campaign, that Labor asked voters what impact they thought One Nation would have on election day.

If you think the main political parties don't use the word 'racism' in their polling, get ready to open your mind. One in three voters who were questioned (34 per cent) thought One Nation was 'a dangerous development that has introduced racism and prejudice into Australian politics'. The majority (55 per cent) said that One Nation was 'sending a message to the major parties that Ordinary Australians [sic] should get a fair go at last'. Another 6 per cent answered 'yes' to both propositions. For what it's worth, the Queensland republican vote was 37.44 per cent in 1999, the nation's lowest, and the only return below 40 per cent.

Yet, at the start of 2001, Queensland had been 'de-red necked' in one important respect. One Nation supporters — who Labor and the coalition were now dubbing 'Hansonites' — were not as angry about race as they had been in the late 1990s. In its regular tracking surveys, Labor asked Queenslanders to identify two issues, from a list of fourteen, that 'are the most important to you in deciding' who gets your vote. Overall, 'Aboriginal issues' ranked last, receiving a mention from only from 1 per cent of soft voters, 1 per cent of Liberal supporters, and 2 per cent of One Nation supporters. This contrasted with the Wik cacophony of 1997–8 when 'native title' rated as a top-six priority for voters generally — behind jobs, education, health, crime, and the environment, but ahead of 'open and honest government', and 'taxes and charges'.

This shift in sentiment in Queensland, from indignant to indifferent on Australian Aboriginal issues, is one of the revelations of our times. From one perspective, it shows that the electorate is not overtly racist. The focus groups that Labor and Liberal use to test the mindset of the community tends to be an echo chamber. Prejudice is rarely volunteered. Rather, it surges and wanes like water rushing into a blowhole, spraying into view only after politicians and opinion-makers in the media have been arguing about race. Native title was a hot topic in Queensland in 1997–8 precisely because Howard, Hanson, and Borbidge were leading the chorus. But after Howard reached his Wik compromise with Tasmanian independent senator Brian Harradine, the coalition promptly dropped the subject. The temperature thus lowered, the One Nation voter would find other things to become anxious about. Not even Hanson could convince them to revive the fear and loathing that had been directed towards Australian Aboriginals.

A paradox of 2001 is that while 40 per cent of Queensland voters saw One Nation as 'introducing racism and prejudice into Australian politics', the Queensland One Nation voter was not motivated by race at the state election. To put the lack of interest of the One Nation voter about Australian Aboriginal issues in perspective, the only topics of less concern to them were the environment and the economy, rating at 1 per cent each.

The Hansonites are outcasts in the truest sense of the word. So removed are they from the values of the new middle class in the inner cities, or the middle-aged class in quarter-acre suburbia, that they don't care whether the economy grows or slips into recession. Interest rates don't rate as a policy concern if you don't have a mortgage, nor does the direction of GDP if you don't have a job. The Labor pollsters found One Nation voters in Queensland were less motivated generally by the bread-and-butter worries of middle Australia: employment, health, and education. They were more concerned about crime, fuel prices, and road transport.

The Hansonite, as Labor research leading up to the 2001 federal election shows, is more likely to be male, over 50, working class, and on an income of $30,000 a year or less. This mirrors research that the coalition has conducted.[2] One of One Nation's myths is that it was a party of the bush. In fact, Hanson's main supporters were more likely to be found in the outer suburbs rather on the land. The farmer who trades in the global economy has, in fact, more in common with the values of new Australia. None of this would amount to much if Australia didn't have a compulsory voting system. In the United States, the equivalent of the Hansonite wouldn't bother showing up on polling day. Here, though, these citizens can decide marginal seats. It is their rejection of mainstream politics that is the key. Even today, long after Hanson's departure, the main parties agree that the Hansonite is pivotal because 'he' has no residual loyalty to the main parties. He is the 'wanted voter' whose poster is pinned in campaign headquarters federally, and in the state branches of Queensland, New South Wales, and Western Australia.

* * *

One Nation polled 22.7 per cent of the primary vote at its debut at the 1998 Queensland state election. Labor calculated that one-third came from Labor and two-thirds from the coalition — a defection from mainstream politics of roughly 7 per cent away from Labor, and 14 per cent away from the coalition. As a first-up message from old Australia to new Australia, it was the middle finger. But it could have been an even bigger statement. According to a secret post-election report given to Beattie in 1998, if Labor had also courted One Nation instead of placing it last on party how-to-vote cards, 'One Nation would now hold 20 seats — the 11 they actually won, plus the nine coalition seats Labor's preferences saved — in the Queensland parliament'.

Under that scenario, One Nation would have been the main opposition party.

At the federal election later that year, One Nation collected almost one million primary votes — 936,621, or 8.43 per cent of all ballots cast for the house of representatives. Two in every three of these votes — 618,493 — were concentrated in outer-metropolitan and country-town-based federal electorates in Queensland and New South Wales, which happened to be where the bulk of the coalition's vulnerable seats stood. So Howard had every reason to look carefully at the Queensland state election in 2001. As it transpired, the state coalition was routed. The nature of the victory — even One Nation surrendered most of its seats to Labor — prompted Peter Beattie to declare it a triumph for multiculturalism:

> What I am pleased about is that Queenslanders tonight have really voted for a fair go ... One of the great things that makes us great Queenslanders and great Australians is that we judge people on what's in their heart, what sort of people they are, not the colour of their skin or their religion or their gender. And that's what makes us a great nation, that makes us the greatest democracy in the world. I'm committed to multiculturalism. Tonight was a vote for the fair go and that was a good thing.[3]

Within weeks, Howard lost a federal by-election in the previously safe Liberal seat of Ryan, which was one of the two Queensland electorates to vote 'yes' for the republic in 1999. Howard found in Ryan what Beattie found at the state poll: the GST was turning the Liberal heartland over to Labor. The inner city of Brisbane was beginning to take on the characteristics of the southern axis of excess of Sydney, Melbourne, and Canberra. For instance, the once-battling Brisbane suburb of Paddington had caught up with its namesake in Sydney's inner east on the latte index. In early 2001, Brisbane's Paddington had twenty cafes and 45 restaurants listed in the *Yellow Pages*. Sydney's Paddington had twenty-one and 42 respectively. In Canberra, one senior federal cabinet minister told me bluntly that Howard was destroying the Liberal Party. This minister saw the defection of middle-income and higher-income voters in Queensland to Labor as proof that Howard's conservative agenda was nearing its use-by date.[4]

This, then, was life before the publicity of the gang rapes in Sydney, the *Tampa*, and September 11 reignited the politics of race. At the 2001 refugee election, Queensland delivered the second-largest swing to the coalition after New South Wales. Yet the make-up of Australian society, the balance between old men, new women, and immigration, didn't budge between these two polls held in February and November. So what really happened? Did the nation's heart suddenly become harder? Did Howard tap latent prejudice in the community? Or was this merely politics, the public's knee being jerked by the events in August and September 2001? For the latter to be the case, the polls taken before the *Tampa*, and the ones taken after boats stopped coming, should show the electorate focusing on issues other than race. The best place to begin checking the public's pre-*Tampa* pulse is the forum where Howard believes conservative leaders get their best hearing: radio. In a more reflective moment after the election, Howard offered this advice to fellow conservatives at a Washington luncheon:

> Like all democratic nations, I guess Australia is no different in the sense that there is a greater preponderance of people in the media of a — how should I put it mildly and gently and diplomatically — of a centre-left disposition. Talkback radio is tremendously important in Australia, enormously important.

> It has played a greater role in shaping and determining the outcome of elections over the last few years than perhaps has been the case with other sections of the media.[5]

The transcripts of Radio Howard from the start of 2001 allow us to pinpoint when the public began nursing a grudge against asylum-seekers. Howard was involved in 28 talkback interviews in the first three months of 2001. The vote-switching federal issue at the time, which assisted state Labor in Queensland, was petrol prices. It bobbed up virtually every time Howard ventured onto the airwaves. Before the Queensland state election, Howard insisted he could not return the extra GST that was being collected on top of the regular fuel excise. To do so, he told radio listeners repeatedly, would be 'financially irresponsible'. Howard was stubborn because he had another idea in mind for his petrol windfall. His Plan A for re-election was economic management, not border protection. He wanted to deliver personal income-tax cuts in the May budget to neutralise the GST as an issue. But the Queensland poll forced a dramatic reassessment. Howard figured he was running out of time to get the public back on side.

Cornered, he performed a series of backflips that was unprecedented in Australian politics. He gave motorists more than they had expected by abolishing any further indexation of fuel excise. It contradicted everything he stood for as a tax reformer. Howard had preached at the 1998 election that a GST was needed to replace the wholesale sales tax because it was a fairer and more efficient levy. The reasoning was that the money collected by the GST would grow in line with the economy. Sales tax, on the other hand, applied to some goods and not others, and not to services. This narrow base meant sales tax had an annoying tendency of running behind the economy, which forced governments to cover the subsequent budget shortfalls by lifting it from the wallets of workers via the back door of bracket creep. By freezing fuel excise — the federal government's second-largest growth tax after the GST — Howard reduced it to the same status as the old sales tax. As an act of hypocrisy, not to mention 'financial irresponsibility', it took some beating. However, this pragmatist was gambling that taking petrol prices off the radio-talkback switchboard was worth the black hole in the budget.

Howard forked out what remained of Peter Costello's prized surplus to small business, first-home buyers, beer drinkers, pensioners, and self-funded retirees — a poll-driven check list of all the groups that threatened to punt him out of power because of the GST. The kitty thus emptied, neither Howard nor Beazley had any money left to play with at the coming election. It is into this vacuum, where the traditional tax auction was no longer an option, that the scene was set for the war on boat people.

At his nadir, after the loss of the blue-ribbon seat of Ryan, Howard said his government had been 'carpet-bombed'[6] by a run of bad news: defeats at the Western Australian and Queensland state elections; confirmation from the Australian Bureau of Statistics national accounts that the GST had shrunk the economy in the final three months of 2001; and a fall in the dollar. It would get worse. In May came the leaking of a secret report from federal Liberal Party president Shane Stone, telling Howard that he was perceived as running a 'mean, tricky and dysfunctional' government.[7] In August, disgruntled Liberal Party members showered Labor with details of a GST fiddle that implicated the then small business minister, Ian Macfarlane, member for the southern Queensland seat of Groom. The last press release Howard issued before the *Tampa* called on Labor to refer any evidence it had in the Macfarlane case to the Australian Taxation Office.[8]

After seven months of unrelenting gloom for the government, the *Tampa* seemed to come as an act of divine intervention. It was Howard's reverse carpet-bomb, wiping all other debates off the political horizon. The public response was overwhelming. The issue played out like a national law-and-order campaign, a scare tactic normally associated with desperate state oppositions. The 2001 refugee election was held in the frightening weeks after September 11, when time seemed to be measured in anthrax scares. It was the first election in more than a generation that did not have an economic issue at its heart. For a parallel, you have to look back to the communist scares of the 1950s, when Robert Menzies played the Petrov card after KGB agent Vladimir and his wife Evdokia defected in stranger-than-Hollywood circumstances in 1954. At the time, Labor had been confident of reclaiming power federally. It was already dominant at the state level, forming governments in every jurisdiction except South Australia. But the Petrov affair, like the *Tampa,* eclipsed all other topics. Menzies called a snap election on the back of the defection, and won. But, unlike Howard, he lost the two-party vote to Labor by 49.3 to 50.7 per cent.

Even with the benefit of hindsight, it is difficult to detect from Radio Howard transcripts that asylum-seekers were on his mind for anything more than a month before the confrontation with the *Tampa*. In his first 28 radio interviews between January and March, as 17 vessels deposited asylum-seekers on Australian soil, Howard received no direct questions on boat people.[9] A lone Perth radio listener rang on 7 February to offer Howard a pat on the back for his general stance on reconciliation and refugees. Howard replied:

> Well, I can understand that and I thank you Lynette for what you said. I appreciate the expression of support ... but I don't want anyone to run away with the idea that people are harshly treated. But equally you cannot come here as an illegal

> immigrant, without permission, and then expect to be treated as an ordinary member of society. I mean you have to have some detention while your status is being clarified. And I think when you look around the world, we've handled this very difficult issue in a very humanitarian fashion.

There was no sign here that he would stop all boats from landing. The opening two questions came in April, as riots in detention centres gained media coverage. Again, one could be forgiven for thinking that Howard believed the system was working. On 6 April, he said:

> You can't accept people who come here illegally then getting [sic] away with trashing property and rioting and defying authority. On the other hand, you are dealing with a lot of people who fled from very desperate situations who feel persecuted. Some of them have very strong cases to put.

On 12 April, he continued to chart a middle course:

> We have to balance our right to deal with illegal entries into Australia, we've got to balance that against our humanitarian responsibilities not to turn back people into the sea so that they will drown.

Here is the asylum-seeker data of the time. The first seven months of 2001 saw the number of people coming to Australia by boat more than double. Yet the actual numbers — 3687 people versus 1446 for the same period in 2000 — did not suggest the system was stretched to breaking point. Between 3 January and 23 April, 17 boats landed in Australia. Of the human cargo, 1278 were placed in detention and 366 were granted temporary protection visas (which gave them the right to temporarily live among other Australians). In May and June another nine boats came, with 831 sent to detention. But there were no boats in July, the second clear month of the year after February. In August, traffic resumed with six boats carrying 1212 people in total. Then came the *Tampa*, which rescued, at Australia's request, some 433 Afghanis and Iraqis stuck on a sinking vessel.[10]

Timing and luck are two key ingredients in any political operation. If the *Tampa* had turned up a mere fortnight later, after September 11, Howard may well have embraced those fleeing the Taliban and Saddam Hussein, just as public opinion had demanded he help another group of Muslims, the Kosovars, in 1999. Then again, even if we accept the government's argument that the surge in boat-people numbers in the first half of 2001 did constitute a crisis, it seemed to have escaped Howard's favourite shock jock. Sydney's Alan Jones has been publicly credited by the Liberals as having helped secure seats for Howard at the 1998 GST election. Equally, he is accused by the left of playing a crucial role in the 2001 election by whipping up the asylum-seeker issue. In his dealings with Howard, Jones was moved to mention refugees just once in the seven months before the *Tampa*. On 14 May, Jones approached the subject by reading out queries and comments from his listeners:

> **Jones**: Terry asked, 'When are you going to do something?" And I asked him what he meant by 'do something'. 'About the hoons and the hooligans at Port Hedland detention centre'.
>
> **Howard**: Well, we're certainly not going to do what Mr Beazley does and basically side with the people who riot and demonstrate ... These people come here illegally, they are treated humanely, they are treated far more humanely in that detention centre than they were in the country from which they fled.

Jones: A caller asked what would happen if 100 Aussies arrived illegally in say Japan, Thailand, Singapore, or New York and proceeded to cause havoc?

Howard: Well, they would be put in a plane and sent back here.

Jones: So why don't we do that?

Howard: Well, except that we would take them back if they were Australian citizens. Whereas the people that come here illegally, the countries from which they come, won't take them back. That's the problem and that's the critical difference.

This exchange was the first involving Howard to suggest that voters were turning against asylum-seekers, albeit as seen through a straw poll of Jones's old Australia audience. Yet Howard was quick to clarify the point that his government had a moral obligation to look after boat people, because the nations 'from which they fled' did not respect human rights. After the *Tampa*, Howard argued that the rest of the world should share the burden of settling those found to be genuine refugees. Jones, however, did not think asylum-seekers would be the real issue for Howard at the coming election:

Jones: I want to get on to this HIH, but another caller said this ... 'You've given in to the media' — this is you — [the Prime Minister] 'the Labor Party, the wimps in your own party and the National Party in saying that you'll put Pauline Hanson last on Liberal voting tickets'. You know you can't win the election without the Hanson preferences, what are you going to do to get them?

Howard: What I'm going to do is ask potential One Nation voters not to waste their vote, but to vote for us. And to point out that the legitimate concerns they have, and most of the concerns of the One Nation voters are the concerns of

> Australians — they're not bigoted concerns. There are a few people who fall into that category but, and I won't get their support. But the great bulk of people who are attracted to One Nation are concerned about their economic future, they're concerned about the pace of economic change and what I'll be saying to them in order to get their first preference votes is that our policies are better able to address their concerns than the policies of One Nation.

There we have it, out of the mouth of Jones, and the response of Howard. The 2001 election boiled down to who could snag the votes of the losers of economic change, the Hansonites — not their preference vote, but their primary vote, the number '1' they would place on the ballot paper. Howard reasoned by this stage that One Nation supporters could not be relied on to preference the coalition in sufficient numbers ahead of Labor as they had done in 1998.

Just three months earlier, Howard talked to the father of shock jocks, John Laws. The interview was conducted on 19 February, two days after the Queensland state poll. Howard seemed somewhat in awe of what Beattie had achieved. Labor had gone into the campaign rocked with allegations of electoral rorting. Three Labor politicians had resigned in disgrace, including deputy premier Jim Elder. Yet Beattie managed to convince voters that he was 'the only virgin in the brothel', in the words of one Howard strategist. Howard told Laws:

> It looked, on occasions as though [Beattie] were campaigning against the Labor Party as much as he was campaigning against the Liberal and the National Party.

Howard would have been aware that coalition research showed voters judged Beattie as better able to deal with rorting than his National opponent Borbidge, even though it had been Labor caught doing the rorting. Howard then offered Laws his take on what Queensland voters wanted:

> In the end, the public voted for the stability and the security that [Beattie] offered in contrast to a good deal of disunity and aimlessness on the other side. There's no point not calling a spade a spade.

Stability and security were phrases that he re-uttered at the refugee election. But the most revealing comment Howard made that day was about One Nation. Back then, he was still keen for their preferences:

> I think there's too much preoccupation on where the major parties allocate their preferences because our preferences, in all probability, won't be distributed. It's the preferences of the minor parties that get distributed and people who are contemplating voting in any election for a minor party, they have to think about their preferences, especially at a federal level because we have compulsory preferential voting, unlike Queensland which has optional preferential voting. You can't just put '1' in the square in the federal poll.

Thus, somewhere between February and May, between chats with Laws and Jones, Howard decided he couldn't win the federal election unless he could convince One Nation supporters to vote directly for the coalition. This epiphany is one of the keys to understanding what Howard achieved in his refugee election of 2001.

Immigration, like petrol prices, is a vote-switcher. But organisations such as Newspoll can only show this in an oblique way. In 2001, Newspoll ran three issues-based surveys, in January,

June, and September. It rated fifteen areas that the public saw as 'very important' in how they would vote in a federal election. In January 2001, immigration was given a score of 37 per cent, placing it second-last of the fifteen, ahead only of Australian Aboriginals and native title issues, which were at the bottom on 32 per cent. On top of the poll was education (77 per cent), followed by health and Medicare (74 per cent). However, by September 2001, immigration had jumped to ninth place, with 50 per cent rating it as very important. Behind it were defence, interest rates, women's issues, inflation, and industrial relations. Australian Aboriginals and native title issues slipped further still to 29 per cent.

These polls understate the true mood of the electorate. Liberal and Labor strategists admit that education and health are not the big vote-switchers that pundits think. It is only when one side tries something too radical, as the coalition had on Medicare at its doomed GST election of 1993, that concerns with health or education translate into a swing to the other party. In the lead-up to the 2001 campaign, Liberal and Labor tended towards bipartisanship on the big issues. This allowed the real political battle to be engaged at the margin. As late as April–May 2001, immigration did not rate as an issue in the private polling of the main parties, which might explain why Jones didn't detect it on his radar. But immigration sprang up in June — tellingly, before the publicity of the gang rapes in Sydney. The resentment in the electorate was aimed at asylum-seekers, not those refugees who were already settled here. 'Race had replaced inequality as the main concern of the working class', was how one main party strategist put it. The trigger was not so much the boats arriving at the time, but the riots in detention centres.

In focus groups, voters began parroting the lines they were picking up from politicians and the media: people in detention centres were enjoying five-star accommodation. This is akin to the earlier complaint that the working class in Queensland had with Australian Aboriginals. After the *Tampa*, it wasn't merely deportation that some punters saw as the solution to greedy asylum-seekers, but something more drastic — 'sink the boats'.

* * *

This is what the power of the refugee card would have looked like to Howard. In the nail-biting weeks between September 11 and the start of the 2001 federal election, the Liberal Party ran a series of focus groups to fine-tune its campaign pitch. One of the voters who helped reassure the Howard government that it was on the right track was a refugee. 'There was a woman, a Palestinian woman, in one of the focus groups', a coalition source said. It's not clear if the other focus group members knew her background because the unprompted discussion quickly assumed an anti-Muslim tone, as voters wrestled with the meaning of the terror attacks on New York, Washington, and Pennsylvania. The refugee spoke out. 'She ripped into them a bit because she felt some people within the group were attacking Islam', the source close to Howard said. The voter declared:

> I live in Australia, I love Australia. [September 11] is not about Islam versus Christianity, it's about terrorists who are fanatics, and fanatics of any type are bad.

Later the talk moved to the Prime Minister's 27 August decision to turn back the *Tampa*. The punters appeared to have little sympathy for boat people. The refugee again became agitated, only this time she was at one with the other voters. She wasn't a queue-jumper; she came here through regular immigration channels after waiting for a number of years. 'She said Howard was right, a country needs to decide who comes into the country and the circumstances', the source said. So the most potent line in Howard's campaign — 'We decide who comes to this country and the circumstances in which they come' — was endorsed a month before he even used it, and from the sort of person he might have worried most about offending. Howard insists that his remark was off-the-cuff. He says he didn't take his cue from the refugee.[11]

Yet Howard would have known when he used the phrase in the second-last week of the campaign that he had the public on side. It featured in the Liberal's advertising blitz, and was quoted on posters and pamphlets that confronted voters as they approached polling booths on election day. That line — which Howard had once criticised as being 'fairly short on liberalism and fairly strong on opportunism' — was powerful enough to define his back-from-the-GST-dead victory.

On election day, the Prime Minister was pressing flesh in his home base of Bennelong when two Sri Lankan women approached him with a similar message to that of the refugee woman two months earlier:

> They said: 'We strongly agree with you because we are trying to get our relatives and parents in through the regular way and we can't and we don't like people pushing their way in.' That may be a simplistic way of putting it, but that's quite a strongly held view and it is quite hard, I find that at an electoral level, it is quite hard to get people in because we have shifted the balance [towards skilled immigrants].[12]

There is no mistaking the popular appeal of Howard's war on boat people. Kim Beazley admitted after the election that Howard's basic proposition — that Australia should not have to accept asylum-seekers who have already found a 'secured haven' in a third country — was supported by 90 per cent of voters. 'And they are right to think so', Beazley said.[13] Labor is certain the refugee issue cost it the election. Liberal campaign director Lynton Crosby disagrees, saying the '*Tampa* had the effect of reinforcing in the minds of the Australian people the existing qualitative difference between John Howard and Kim Beazley'. Immediately after the election, Crosby released a poll into why people voted Liberal. It revealed more than he may have intended because it showed, in fact, how the boat people got Howard home. Crosby said the most common reason for supporting the government, cited by 29 per cent, was 'a longstanding commitment to the Liberal Party/opposition to the Labor Party'. Next were 22 per cent who voted on economic and financial management, followed by 18 per cent who preferred Howard's leadership. Fourth, at 14 per cent, was the government's track record and, fifth, 11 per cent who didn't like Beazley. That left 'illegal entrants/boat people' in sixth place, with 10 per cent.[14]

That figure of 10 per cent is pivotal in the context of an election that was ultimately decided by a few thousand votes over a handful of seats. Crosby didn't say where this 10 per cent came from, but it's not hard to work out. The Hansonite, as we have seen, isn't fussed about economic and financial management, and certainly doesn't believe the government has a good track record. So it stands to reason that the Hansonite was swayed by other issues. Border protection is a safe bet.

In 1998, Howard was returned with a majority of just twelve seats in a parliament of 150. Since the end of the Vietnam War, every newly elected federal government has seen its vote fall at its second and third elections. Labor's Gough Whitlam was the most extreme case, winning in 1972, limping back in 1974, then being slaughtered in 1975. Malcolm Fraser's coalition saw its vote drop in 1977 and 1980 before being toppled in 1983. Bob

Hawke stretched this process even further, with Labor's vote falling steadily in 1984, 1987, and then 1990, where it lost the two-party preferred vote but won a majority of seats. The only exception was Paul Keating, who increased the government's vote in 1993. Yet that was his first election as prime minister. He was turfed out at his second. In 1998, Howard won like Hawke had in 1990, with a minority of the two-party preferred vote. In 2001, history pointed towards defeat for Howard. In defying the odds to win his third straight election with a swing to the government, Howard repeated Keating's first-up effort.

What further binds the 1993 and 2001 polls is that both saw a block of voters who had threatened to swing the election jump back to the government on the strength of a fear card. Keating's was Medicare, which gave him a crucial number of conservative women voters who had earlier wanted to turf him out over the recession. Howard's was the *Tampa*, which turned Labor battlers and Hansonites angry at the GST into coalition primary voters. The former didn't deliver any extra seats to Howard; they only lowered Labor's heartland vote. Labor bled a second round of votes, its pro-refugee middle class in the inner city, which went to the Australian Greens in Melbourne and Sydney. But this did not affect the final result because these protest ballots returned to Labor as preferences. It was the Hansonites, dwelling in old Australia, who decided the election.

Here is where the Hansonites delivered for Howard. Going into the 2001 refugee election, there were 21 marginal federal seats where the Hansonites mattered — eleven in Queensland and ten in New South Wales. Eight in each state were held by the coalition, and would have fallen to Labor with a swing of less than 5 per cent. Labor had the other five. In the 1998 GST poll, the One Nation primary vote in these electorates ranged from 8.3 per cent in Paterson, on the NSW central coast, to 26.3 per cent in Wide Bay, the impoverished seat north of Noosa in

Queensland. It is in this cluster that the bulk of the original one million Hansonites could be found. So what happened to these seats at the 'we decide' poll? In virtually every electorate — eighteen out of 21 — the One Nation vote halved and the coalition primary vote picked up by an almost identical level. Not surprisingly, the coalition held all sixteen Hansonite marginals — some now considered safe — and picked up three of Labor's five.[15]

What sets apart these seats from the rest of the nation is their 'whiteness'. All 21 in the Hansonite belt have more Australian-born voters than the national total of 73 per cent. By extension, there were fewer Australian-born offspring of immigrants in these seats than the Australian average. Most (twelve of 21) have Australian-born populations of 80 per cent or higher. Their outcast status is reinforced by numbers on income and age — seventeen of 21 are below the median family income of $1048 a week ($54,496 a year), and fifteen of 21 are older than the national median age of 35 years. In short, they are the 'WW' electorates — white (by skin and by hair colour) and on welfare. They all voted for the monarchy in 1999.[16]

Take the electorate of Herbert, which is centred around Townsville, the working-class town where Labor first detected a worrying anti-Australian Aboriginal sentiment at the end of 1997. The government held Herbert by just 150 votes in 1998, making it the nation's most marginal seat. Labor was on track to win this seat comfortably before the *Tampa*. Its primary vote was above 40 per cent, the threshold that strategists on both sides agreed should translate to victory for Labor after the distribution of preferences. The two-party vote showed a swing of around 5 per cent to Labor, based on internal research. After the *Tampa*, the scorecard flipped: Labor's primary vote collapsed to the low-thirties, and the Liberal primary vote jumped to the mid-forties. Labor was never in the race for Herbert from that point on. On election day in Herbert, the One Nation primary vote halved from 14.3 per cent to 7.1 per cent. The Liberal primary vote increased by 3.1 per cent to just under 43 per cent, a springboard to a relatively easy win. The final margin was 2665 votes. Herbert is one of the nation's 50 'whitest' electorates, ranked 36th, with an Australian-born population of 83 per cent in August 2001. It is also in the bottom 50 by income at number 41, with a median family income of $963 a week ($50,076 a year). The coalition holds 32 of the 50 'whitest' and, coincidently, 32 of the 50 poorest seats in federal parliament.

Labor polling says it was border protection that brought the Hansonites back to Howard — a point not necessarily disputed by Liberals. 'What Pauline Hanson provided and what John Howard's action in relation to *Tampa* did was give people empowerment — "Good on John Howard, he's standing up for Australia's interests" as they perceived them to be', another coalition source said. 'Now it wasn't racist, it wasn't about race, it was about a concern that we can't even decide who comes here.' This is splitting hairs. It was about race. Without the *Tampa*, the Hansonites still would have been in a mood to unseat the Howard government. This is why politics will be forced to pay closer attention to Generation W when Howard is gone, because the bottom 50 seats will not have someone to bind them to the party of economic rationalism. In these circumstances, new Australians will stand alongside the Hansonites as swinging voters to be reckoned with because the Liberal Party will need to find additional supporters in the middle class to insure against the return of the battlers to Labor.

Where the details get devilish for Labor is what the overall result says about its claim as the party of tolerance. Clearly, there were not enough people offended by Howard's refugee card to offset his partial annexation of the Hansonites. The republic 'yes' seats in Sydney registered swings *to* the government, not against it. Polling by both sides showed that many people thought Beazley would soften his approach to asylum-seekers if he became prime minister. This is an important perception. In 1996, Labor accused Howard of having a hidden agenda to slash government spending — a view shared by voters — but he still won in an avalanche. In 2001, Beazley's hidden agenda appeared to be more dangerous to the electorate. The *Tampa* crystallised the public's view of Beazley as a flip-flopper. One of the ironies is that voters told the main parties that they supported the Howard government's mandatory-detention policy for boat people when it was, in fact, Labor that had installed the razor wire a decade earlier.

The detailed and secret research into why people changed their vote from Labor to the coalition found 'leadership' and 'immigration/refugees' were the only two issues on the radar. September 11, for instance, was not seen as a vote switcher, because voters felt that both the coalition and Labor would pursue the national interest. It was on the specifics of border protection, not the spectre of terrorism, that Labor was rejected. Beazley was seen as 'not strong enough; not up to it; a knocker who changes his mind', according to the most sensitive polling conducted in the middle of the campaign. This document also identified 'women; middle and upper class voters' as being against Labor's policy on the *Tampa*. The Hansonites may have tipped the balance back in Howard's favour, but their attitude towards refugees was in line with what much of new Australia was also thinking. Why women? The gang rapes played a part in Sydney by increasing the public's suspicion of asylum-seekers, according to party sources. The racism report cited in chapter three also found 'Muslim antipathy [was] stronger among female respondents'.

Nonetheless, the majority of the electorate voted for reasons other than refugees. The 2001 result still bewilders Labor today because, before the *Tampa*, it took victory for granted. This arrogance was compounded by a delusion after the election: that the majority of Australians must have been racists to have granted Howard victory. The reverse is true. By arranging the 150 seats in federal parliament by family income we can see why. The coalition won the majority of the bottom and the top fifty, while Labor claimed the middle fifty. Howard's final margin of sixteen, coincidently, comprises the six poorest and the ten wealthiest electorates in the nation. These bottom six seats were influenced by the refugee card. But the top ten seats, comprising eight in Sydney and two in Melbourne, are where the most politically correct Australians are found. So it can't be said that racism ran across the nation.

The 2001 election was evenly poised everywhere else, from seats numbered eleven to 144.[17] This is the most redeeming piece of data, the pointer that the nation is not as intolerant as some might fear. The best way to demonstrate this is to consider what good the *Tampa* would have been for Howard if Labor had been rated by voters as a better economic manager. He would have lost, and Beazley would have been hailing, like Beattie before him, the triumph of a multicultural nation. Australia was never that PC to begin with, nor that prejudiced at the end of 2001. The *Tampa* certainly helped Howard over the line, but the reasons it appealed to the Hansonites were not shared by the rest of the nation. Ordinary Australians had more mundane concerns — for instance, how to keep their house prices from defying the laws of gravity.

In June 2003, a mere two years after the main parties detected the first stirrings of an anti-refugee mood in the electorate, Newspoll ran another of its issues-based surveys. No boats had appeared for eighteen months. Immigration had returned to where it was at the start of 2001, when Howard was on the nose. It was rated as 'very important' by just 38 per cent of voters, placing it alongside inflation and only ahead of industrial relations, and Australian Aboriginal and native title issues. By this time, Howard showed every intention of contesting the next election on other policies, in particular the conundrum of work–family. Labor, on the other hand, was still fighting over the last election.

* * *

In the month that the immigration issue was losing its sting, Melbourne played host to the most emotional sporting event since Cathy Freeman's gold-medal-winning 400 metres race at the 2000 Sydney Olympics. Richmond Football Club faced the Kangaroos on a Friday night to kick off round eleven of the 2003 AFL season. The game marked both the comeback and retirement of a previously unremarkable footballer. Jason McCartney was almost killed in Bali in October 2002, the first act of mass terror to target Australians in the region. His return to the field, after recovering from life-threatening burns to most of his body, was a genuine moment of catharsis. Tiger fans stood and applauded his entry to the ground in the second quarter, and most were still clapping when he helped his side steal a three-point victory in the gripping final seconds of the match.

Of the 202 murdered in Bali, 88 were Australians. Before Bali, relations between the Australian and Indonesian governments were like those of two high-maintenance children in full tanty mode. Sometimes they swapped cold stares and shoulders; on other occasions, they called each other silly names. The initial disagreement was real, over East Timor, and there can be no doubting that Australia held the moral high ground there. But in 2001 it was boat people, and neither side had anything to be proud of. Between Indonesia's disdain and Australia's demonising of asylum-seekers, we caught a glimpse of the darker side of politicians in both nations. After Bali, the refugee card suddenly did not seem so pertinent for either government. There was a real security scare to face, and it required co-operation from the top down. Australian federal police were welcomed by Indonesian authorities as they tracked down the Bali bombers.

In August and September 2001, the nation's insecurity translated into what has since been described as Islamophobia. This is a powerful word, but a misleading one. After Bali, the Howard government was at pains to make the distinction between the moderate Muslim and the extremist. The Prime Minister was keen to be Indonesia's friend and ally in the war against terror. It is against this backdrop, with the risk of more bombs exploding on our doorstep, that the decline in immigration as an issue by mid-2003 is important. It suggests that Australians are more tolerant than their politicians have given them credit for. If immigration reappears as a hot topic, we now know who to blame.

CHAOS THEORY, 2003

POSTSCRIPT

Iraq

AUSTRALIA'S PARLIAMENT HOUSE was designed to serve a laconic democracy: an open door for an open nation. From afar, it seemed as if the building had been dug into the side of Capital Hill. The grassed roof that created this illusion beckoned the public to climb over the top of it and stand over the 226 members and senators in the chambers below. Yet its egalitarian architecture also encouraged one of the most unlikely protests held in any seat of power. In 1992, a pensioner drove his Pajero up to the main entrance, bumped open the glass doors, and parked it in the great marble hall. Fortunately, no one was hurt.

The insider's parliament carries many extra attractions not available to the regular tourist. There is the pampered precinct, where an in-house gymnasium, hairdresser, coffee shop, and travel agency can be found. Nearby is the lift that takes you to a secret floor marked 'M': the meditation room.

One Sunday morning in 1992, I showed a Jewish couple some of the quirks of my workplace. She had grown up in the same neighbourhood as I had in Caulfield; he was from Tel Aviv. As we passed the prime minister's office, I caught a glimpse of the elongated figure of Paul Keating, his back turned to us, in deep conversation with an adviser. I told my buddies that they should discreetly record the moment on their camera so they would have something to show their children. But they had to do it quickly, before Keating noticed, and before one of his attendants bobbed up to stop them. In the meantime I figured I should hide around the corner so the PM wouldn't see who was directing this scene. The Israeli was like a teen with a backstage pass to a rock concert. 'I can't believe it, I am filming the prime minister of Australia', he whispered into the microphone as his video whirred. A guard arrived on cue. I stepped forward, apologised on their behalf, and promised to frogmarch them to a less sensitive zone.

Two years later, my friends had settled in Israel, and it was my turn to play guest. Driving from Tel Aviv to Jerusalem, the Israeli pointed out his nation's parliament along the way. He joked that we would be shot if we tried the same stunt here. I asked if we could stop to pay a visit. 'Are you kidding? They don't let the public walk in off the street', he mocked. It was pretty obvious why. Tanks kept watch on all approaches to the building. Now I could see why his unremarkable encounter with Keating had made such an impression.

The following week, I was in Jerusalem with a fizzy-haired Australian buddy. At the Mount of Olives, in the Arab section overlooking the old city, we paused to pose for silly photos. My friend had a habit of pointing every time she stood in front of a camera. This time she wanted to record the detail in a waist-high wall between a cemetery and us. Chunks of broken glass were cemented across the top to deter anyone who thought of climbing over it. While we dithered over where she would stand, a group of young Palestinian men approached us with the half-menace, half-swagger that is the calling card of security staff in any jurisdiction. 'You can't got there, it's a holy site', one of the Palestinians said. 'We know, we just wanted to take a photo', I offered. 'You American?' another asked. 'No, we're from Australia'. The sneers turned to smiles. 'Ah, I have a cousin in Fremantle. Do you know Fremantle?'

Almost a decade on, and Australia's parliament would look

more like the Israeli's to the Jewish couple. The grassed roof that we had walked over and the road that circled the building have been cordoned off with the chunky white water barriers that you see on freeway construction sites. Every person who enters parliament today, from a member of the public to a pass-holder, faces a metal detector for themselves and an x-ray machine for their belongings. The clampdown, improvised after the Bali bombing, is a metaphor for the exponentially more dangerous times that we live in.

* * *

We began the new millennium as host of the best-ever Olympics. But we became the harasser of asylum-seekers barely a year later, in seeming anticipation of the violence that was to follow. The twin terror-shocks of 11 September 2001 and 12 October 2002 seemed to confirm our mood-swing from optimism to paranoia. Our transformation from welcoming nation to warrior state was completed in March 2003 when we joined the United States and Great Britain in the west's first war of pre-emption; which is jargon for an invasion without a clear-cut threat of attack from the other side.

John Howard gave two essential arguments for Australia joining the US–British forces in Iraq. The first was that Saddam Hussein had to be rid of his chemical and biological weapons. The second factor, he said, and 'unapologetically so, [was] our alliance with the US':

> Alliances are two-way processes and our alliance with the United States is no exception. Australians should always remember that no nation is more important to our longer-term security than that of the United States.[1]

This was certainly true of World War II, when Labor prime minister John Curtin swapped Britain for the United States as our protector-in-chief. But our superpower pal is suddenly more vulnerable because it can't get a fix on its new enemy. The United States and Australia have caught a glimpse of the world that Israelis and Palestinians, British and Irish, Spanish and Basque — in fact, almost every European, Middle Eastern, Asian, African, and Latin American nation — have inhabited for the worst part of a century. It is a place where fanaticism and technology can fuse to commit mass murder. Global terror is recasting the politics of Australia at a time when Generation W is quietly remodelling the nation.

On one level, we are being taken back to the 1950s, when we saw our regional neighbourhood as something to be feared. Yet this is also the moment when our community has never been more cosmopolitan, and our economy has never been more reliant on the rest of the world. Race and sex are non-issues to most Australians under 40, because it is second nature for them to see women and the children of immigrants succeeding. They also accept, without thinking, the dynamic of the Keating–Howard economy: the idea that the nation has to compete to survive. In our region, the two powers we felt most threatened by in the last century, first Japan, then China, long ago reinvented themselves as our practical allies in commerce. The tension between the politicians' urge to serve the new US militarism and the public's instinct for internationalism will be one of the defining issues for Australia.

The debate we need to confront is whether we are getting so close to the United States that people such as the Palestinians whom I bantered with in Jerusalem a decade ago will no longer see the difference. What they liked about us then is what we still take for granted today: our openness. Australia's immigration program is the distinguishing feature that allows a nation of almost 20 million people to matter on a planet of more than six billion. But if the rest of the world increasingly sees the United States as a bully, where will that leave us as its unquestioning friend in the future?

The quality that we always thought we had over North Americans was our ability to get along with people. The reason an Australian traveller elicits a warmer response than a North American is that the rest of the world not only relates to us, it is related to us. The August 2001 census shows that 27 per cent of the Australian population was born overseas. Another 20 per cent are the Australian-born offspring of immigrants, based on the Howard government's estimates. Thus, 47 per cent of our nation has a direct connection to the rest of the world. Yet we risk acquiring the disease of United States insularity. Remember, the United States is an immigrant nation just like ours. But prosperity made its citizens selfish long ago. Their seeming naivety about world affairs, and their delusion that a few precision bombs will eliminate a problem, is the arrogance of affluence. We displayed this very character trait in our attitude to the people who fled the terror states of Afghanistan and Iraq in 2001. We didn't give these people a mere cold shoulder, but a calculated hip and shoulder. Enough voters to decide a federal election applauded the Howard government's decision to use the navy to transport asylum-seekers to bankrupt Pacific atolls. The majority of the population, meanwhile, turned to the property section of the newspaper to see how far above the reserve price their neighbour's house had just sold for.

By the end of July 2003, 51 boat people, including nine children, were still held on Nauru and the Manus Islands despite being assessed as genuine refugees. More than half this group, 29, had come in on the *Tampa* almost two years earlier. Their incarceration was political. The Howard government wanted to avoid the embarrassment of accepting the very people it had tried to make an example of in 2001. No society that values the rule of law should tolerate a situation where refugees are detained for a nanosecond after they have proved their case. Yet these people were prisoners for almost two years, including the year after their claims for refugee status had been accepted by Australian and United Nations' officials. In case some voters have forgotten the meaning of the word 'refugee', the Howard government agreed that these people faced persecution or death in their homelands. The story was broken by Mike Steketee, of the *Australian*. It should have triggered a media uproar.[2] However, by week's end, the issue that dominated the press was the nation's so-called housing-affordability crisis.

The contradiction of Australia today was reaffirmed by our roller-coaster attitude to the war in Iraq. Before the invasion, published opinion polls showed it to be the most unpopular military engagement in our history. As bombs began raining on Baghdad in March 2003, just 51 per cent of the electorate was on side. By contrast, the first US-led Gulf War in 1991 enjoyed 69 per cent support. To compare, the approval rating for the Vietnam War at its outset in 1965 was 52 per cent; the East Timor peacekeeping mission in 1999 was backed by 77 per cent; and the war in Afghanistan in 2001 had 66 per cent in favour.[3] Yet Australians remain fiercely patriotic. A hero's welcome was given to the soldiers who returned home, without them or their allies having found proof that Saddam Hussein possessed weapons of mass destruction. The lesson of the Vietnam conflict was heeded; the nation was now mature enough to disagree on whether to fight, but would not take it out on our troops. A nation that is fifty-fifty about war cannot claim to be united, no matter how dominant the government of the day might be. Unlike the *Tampa*, the fourth R — regime change in Iraq — was a war for which the Howard government worried it would not win community endorsement. What the government was most nervous about was being seen as a lackey of the United States. Howard betrayed his sensitivity in the mixed responses he gave to three specific invitations from US President George W. Bush before, during, and after the invasion. At the start of February 2003, with war still six weeks away, and public opinion still against him, Howard suddenly hopped on a plane to Washington. Quizzed as to why he needed to see Bush in person when they had just spoken on the phone, Howard replied:

> Personal discussions always have a greater impact than discussions over the phone. That is why people see each other instead of conducting all of their business over the phone.[4]

In late March, with the war then a few days old, Bush offered his allies a second face-to-face briefing. This time, however, Howard did not see the point in meeting with Bush. By contrast, British Prime Minister Tony Blair took the next flight out of London. Of all the linguistic gyrations Howard executed on Iraq, the most revealing during this sensitive period was his transformation from visitor of the willing to desk bound in Australia. Responding to a sarcastic question from a reporter in Canberra as to why he turned down this particular photo opportunity with Bush and Blair, Howard said:

> Well, I don't live for photo opportunities ... It's an intriguing way of asking the question. No, I don't think I made the wrong call at all. I've had plenty of contact with President Bush. I was in America quite recently. I was in Britain quite recently. I've had regular telephone conversations with them. I'm sure I'll have further bilateral telephone conversations with both of them over the days and weeks ahead. I formed the judgement that right at the moment my responsibility to the Australian people, to the families of those who are serving in the Gulf,

> could be best discharged by my remaining in Australia. I'll have plenty of opportunities to go to the United States. I, in a sense, took a raincheck on it.[5]

Once the battle ended, however, Howard was happy to resume contact in the flesh with Bush. At the start of May, Howard met with Bush and had a sleepover at the presidential ranch in Crawford, Texas. The rainchck in the middle of this trio of presidential hospitality appeared to underline the nervousness within government ranks that Howard could lose politically by being seen with Bush at the wrong time. The context here is pivotal. In late March, it was not yet clear if the war would be a quick, decisive one or a drawn out, street-by-street campaign.

* * *

Our mixed feelings toward the United States are a gut reaction that we should not discount. The United States is defined not just by its military might, but also by its soft power. For the best part of a century, the United States only resorted to arms after it had been fired upon, or had been asked to by world opinion. Iraq broke these twin rules of engagement. Notwithstanding our relief that the most brutal dictator in the Middle East had been removed from his palace, Iraq was a troubling precedent for a democracy to set. Howard seemed to understand this better than the United States president: 'He [the US President] wants regime change. This is an area where our policy is different from America.'[6]

However, that statement of principle was made at the end of January, when Howard still hoped that the United Nations would approve action against Iraq. Six weeks later, when it was clear there would be no rubber stamp, Howard dropped any pretence that Australia and the United States were about to march into battle for conflicting reasons: 'There is also a strong humanitarian argument in favour of seeing regime change in Baghdad', he told Alan Jones.[7]

Later that day, in his address to the National Press Club, Howard resorted, once again, to fudge:

> I couldn't justify, on its own, a military invasion of Iraq to change the regime. I've never advocated that, much in all as I despise the regime. But what I was really trying to say today, and perhaps it had some effect, is that I get a bit tired of the humanitarian argument all being to the one side. It's about time that the humanitarian argument was put in a better balance and people understood what a monstrous regime we are dealing with.[8]

This is one of many examples of Howard's flip-flopping in the weeks before war. It was not one of his better efforts at advocacy in 30 years in politics. It reflected the very real difficulty of explaining why the United States, after a century of promoting the rule of international law, was now shooting first and making up the questions later. Regime change is the antithesis of the 'righteous might' that president Franklin D. Roosevelt talked about in the 1940s.

The triumph that exemplified the true nature of United States strength in the last century was not Normandy, Hiroshima, or Nagasaki but the end of the Cold War. The collapse of the Berlin Wall in 1989, and the dissolution of the Soviet Union soon after, did not require force. The people behind the iron curtain saw the contest as their leaders from Lenin onwards had told them: capitalism versus the planned economy, and democracy versus the one-party state. The people chose freedom over dogma, and brought down our rivals for us. The war on terror is, on one level, a re-run of the Cold War: a clash of ideologies that pits west against east. But this hot war differs in three important respects. First, it is not a conflict between nation states: governments in the west and east are targeted equally by terrorists. Second, the west can't find a common purpose, as the split over how to deal with Iraq demonstrated. And, third is the only thing the west can agree on — the people who want to flee fundamentalism in the east are a nuisance. Here, ironically, Australia has proven to be a world leader as Britain, continental Europe, and even the United States have been implementing their own versions of our border-protection regime since the *Tampa*.

A week before we learned that the Howard government still held 51 genuine refugees in limbo under its Pacific solution, the *New York Times* reported the plight of two Haitian men who were still behind bars in Miami some four months after they had been granted political asylum. This pair was being made to pay for the sins of the Middle East:

> Officials say they are trying to discourage Haitians from migrating illegally to the United States. They say a mass migration of Haitians would require the Coast Guard to focus on interdicting people at seas, diverting precious resources needed to protect the United States in the aftermath of [September 11]. In April, Attorney-General John Ashcroft ruled that Haitians and other illegal immigrants without links to terrorist groups could be detained indefinitely to address such national security concerns. He said the State Department had learned that Haiti had become a staging point for Pakistanis and Palestinians hoping to enter the United States illegally, a charge that has been disputed by advocates for immigrants.[9]

Sound familiar? Those Pakistanis sure do get around. One minute they are impersonating Afghanis on leaky boats off the coast of Western Australia; the next, they are pretending to be

Haitians paddling towards Florida. Never mind the Afghanis, the Iraqis, and the Haitians in between, who get tarred with the Karachi brush. Treating the victim as part of the problem reverses the moral compass of the Cold War, when the right sided with the people behind the iron curtain while the left sympathised with communism.

* * *

The moderate Muslim is the swinging voter in the battle between west and east today in the same way that the Soviet citizen was during the Cold War. There will always be many thousand times more Muslim men and women, from Jerusalem to Jakarta, queuing for visas at United States consulates than would think to join Al Qaeda. Australia's national interest, like the United State's, must always be with those who seek a better life. Otherwise, our immigrant and libertarian societies become self-contradictory. The micro-campaign against boat people and the war in Iraq require twin leaps of faith from Canberra and Washington that the moderate Muslim won't take these gestures personally. Yet if Howard can infuriate almost half the Australian electorate on the issues of asylum-seekers and regime change, how can he expect someone living in a totalitarian Islamic republic to receive a balanced picture of these policies? Howard can't trust the ABC at home to see the world as he does. Surely he doesn't believe Al Jazeera will be more loyal to Australia when it beams its version of the wars on refugees and terror into Muslim living rooms around the world?

The frustration that the United States experienced in stabilising Iraq after Saddam is a reminder that hard power is not an end in itself. What makes the US unique is its soft power, the allure of the free market, the rule of law, motion pictures, and rock 'n' roll. These were the ingredients that enticed those living behind the iron curtain to reject the propaganda of their own rulers.

One of the most endearing images of the fall of communism in eastern Europe was dissident rock fan and playwright Vaclav Havel. On assuming the presidency in Czechoslovakia in 1989, Havel invited the Rolling Stones to play a concert in Prague, and appointed cult musician Frank Zappa as his adviser on the United States. This was soft power as the power of song. Today, the pop contest has switched to Iran, the birthplace of Islamic fundamentalism and the anti-US chant, 'death to Satan', where two-thirds of the population is aged under 30 years. In 2001, the ayatollahs were forced to lift their 22-year ban on western music. Iranian clerics promoted local acts such as Shadmehr Aghili as an antidote to Eminem and Britney Spears, whose bootleg recordings were top of the charts in Teheran's black market. This echoed the ham-fisted response of the old Soviet Union, which thought that the state-sponsored art it dubbed 'socialist realism' could stop kids listening to Elvis Presley.

Hard power, when exercised as revenge, and without the evidence to back it up, can make the United States weaker, not stronger, by reducing its soft power. Australia does not help its cause when it is seen to be too close to the United States. By the end of July, with the war won but peace some years away, the Bush and Blair governments came under pressure from their own voters for over-hyping the case for war. Australians also felt deceived. Newspoll found that two out three voters (67 per cent) said that the Howard government 'misled, knowingly or unknowingly, the Australian public about whether Iraq had weapons of mass destruction'. This turned the tables on an earlier survey at the start of February, when three in four (75 per cent) agreed that Iraq had weapons of mass destruction.[10] Howard used that first poll to argue the case for war:

> There is overwhelming evidence that Iraq has chemical and

> biological weapons and [although] I'm not being driven by opinion polls on this issue, as you'll acknowledge, according to all the polls 75 per cent of all Australians believe Iraq has chemical and biological weapons.[11]

So the opposite finding, that public opinion was now strongly the other way, should have ruffled Howard. But it didn't. Instead, he took many more words to explain why his position had not been damaged by the public's assessment that it had been told a whopper on weapons of mass destruction:

> What the poll said, it's interesting if people have a look at it, is not all that surprising. What it said was that 36 per cent thought they had been deliberately misled, which is exactly the same number of people who in the final Newspoll on participation in the war [taken in mid-April] opposed Australia's participation.[12]

Note carefully how he switches the next-largest number in the July weapons-of-mass-destruction poll with the smallest:

> Twenty-five per cent said they did not think they had been misled knowingly or unknowingly, and 31 per cent said they thought they had been unknowingly misled. And, interestingly, those two together is almost identical to the total number of people who supported our involvement in the war.

The final Newspoll he referred to was conducted in mid-April, immediately after the defining, stage-managed image of the war's end was beamed into Australian living rooms — the toppling of Saddam's statue in Baghdad. Those for Australian involvement numbered 57 per cent; those against, 36 per cent. This poll did not ask about weapons of mass destruction.[13] The response from Howard in late July is one of the most revealing of his post-*Tampa* phase. It is, in fact, his take on how many Australians don't like him. Government insiders have, in the past, referred to the 'Howard haters' in the community. The right sees this bloc of roughly 40 per cent of the electorate as the same one that rejected Howard on the three Rs of republic, reconciliation, and refugees. By this calculus, the contest at the ballot box is for the 60 per cent of the population that comprise Howard's rusted-on supporters, together with the swingers.

'There were [also] big numbers marching on reconciliation', a source close to Howard told me after Australian troops were welcomed home from Iraq without casualty. 'I think there's a group of people who look for opportunities; they are frustrated with conservative government.'

When I ran my concept of Generation W past a former Howard cabinet minister, he replied that most professional women and many of the children of immigrants were too busy or too apathetic to favour either Liberal, Labor, Democrats, or Greens. They may be perceptive enough to see that the government misled them on the justification for war, he said, but that would not necessarily stop them from voting Liberal in the future. Twenty-somethings in particular have not known recession in their working lives. This group was more 'me-focused' than those who came before them, the senior conservative said.

Iraq, like the three Rs before it, was an example of poor leadership: from Labor. A party that does not offer a viable alternative cannot expect the public to rise above their everyday concerns to make a moral call on an issue as basic as the case for going to war. The poll that showed 67 per cent of voters thought they had been misled on weapons of mass destruction, whether deliberately or not, also had 59 per cent preferring Howard to Simon Crean as prime minister. In fact, on the eve of his 64th birthday, Howard still enjoyed a 40-point lead on Crean and the coalition — a 10-point lead over Labor.

The idea that voters can support a government that may have fibbed to them is not new, and is not confined to conservative prime ministers. Australians have a history of sticking with governments after their credibility has been tarnished. The process began with the 'Little Digger', Labor defector Billy Hughes, who split the nation in half with his two failed attempts to introduce conscription for World War I, in 1916 and 1917. Yet he won a federal election in between. The Vietnam War was on the nose with public opinion in 1969, yet John Gorton's coalition government prevailed at the ballot box. The 'fistful of dollars' tax cuts that Malcolm Fraser offered in 1977, then cancelled after the poll, did not prevent him from a winning another term in 1980. Labor, in turn, survived two losable elections, Bob Hawke's in 1990, and Paul Keating's in 1993, despite the promised soft economic landing turning into hard recession. As late as January 1995, long after his self-described L.A.W. tax cuts had been dishonoured, Keating still enjoyed a 26-point lead over then opposition leader Alexander Downer. Finally, Howard secured a majority of seats, but not votes, in 1998 for the GST he had said would 'never ever' be coalition policy again. All this proves is that the public quickly forgets unloved opposition leaders, and leaves it to history to sort out the prime ministers who defeat them.

* * *

Today Vietnam is not a war that divides the nation. It is a buzz word for a war that was not in our national interest. The ultimate verdict on Iraq will similarly require some years of hindsight. What we do know today is that Australia has a unique opportunity to try to bring the United States back to the position that served it so well during the Cold War, when it was seen as synonymous with the west. But that would require both the coalition and Labor to get over the idea that we need to be an unquestioning ally to secure United States protection. Neither our interests, nor those of the United States, are served if the United States plays by its own rules. In any case, now is not the time to be getting too close to the United States. The first three years of the new millennium saw Australia defy a United States recession. Our economy continued growing, and the Howard government kept the budget in surplus, while the Bush administration fumbled to restart their economy and allowed the budget to plunge into deficit. This is why the invasion of Iraq was counter-intuitive from Australia's viewpoint. It presupposed that we knew more about the other side of the world than other commonwealth nations such as Canada or New Zealand that remained neutral. We also put ourselves back in the orbit of an economy we no longer relied on to make a buck in the world.

Our security, both physical and economic, cannot be assured through blind loyalty to the United States. Just as we cannot assume that the monarchy will rule eternally in the United Kingdom, we can't take it for granted that the United States will remain on its present course of confrontation. Australia cannot escape its geography. We are a western nation in a region that is both a powder keg and a star of the global economy. Our greatest asset — our ability to absorb people of all cultures and colours — is our strongest weapon. Australia can only claim to be the best part of the world when it is prepared to be a part of it. But that would require knowing when to say 'no' to the United States.

⁂ ⁂ ⁂

Generation W is Australia's double-edged demographic. It sits in the middle of the nation's income table, is located in the centre of the nation's capital cities, and is in the prime of life — the twenties and thirties. It is the least political generation that Australia has known, but it has led the largest rallies we have seen for reconciliation and peace. It is a generation that vindicates the working woman and proves that immigration works, but it is not large enough yet to decide who leads the nation. It has already proved its worth by forcing a conservative government to deal with the reality of the professional woman and to boost the regular immigration intake above 100,000 a year. Its vindication will come with a time lag, in the next decade or so, when one of its own inevitably becomes prime minister and the nation finds an acceptable formula for a republic.

Before then, the challenges for Generation W are the things it marched for: to get the present generation of politicians to advance the cause of reconciliation with our original citizens, and to sort out where we stand in the battle of wills between the United States and Europe. Australia, the nation that reflects the best part of the world back to itself, should move now to break down the communication barriers between the governments of the west and the peoples of the east.

Notes

Introduction

1 Breakdown by region supplied to the *Australian* by the prime minister's office, July 2002. The figures show 18.4 per cent of all people living in Bennelong were Asian-born.

2 As early as February 2002, Newspoll found 62 per cent of voters surveyed thought Hollingworth should resign. Only 22 per cent wanted him to stay on.

3 In 2001, Labor won 30 of the middle 50 electorates in 2001; the Liberal Party, 18; the National Party and independents, one each. In 1998, Labor had 32; Liberals, 16; Nationals and independents, one each. Translation: don't believe the pundit who says the centre is the fount of all political power. The criterion is family income, and the calculations are mine, using unpublished census material supplied to the *Australian* by the Australian Bureau of Statistics in December 2002.

4 Sources: Newspoll, UMR Research, and Australian Gallup Polls.

Chapter One: Generation W

1 Australian Bureau of Statistics' August 2001 census. Numbers have been rounded to the nearest whole number for simplicity. The raw data shows women held 795,479 of the 1,514,096 professional jobs in the economy. Women also claimed 443,276 of the 709,519 bachelor degrees between 1991 and 2001.

2 'Second Generation Australians', press statement and executive

summary, released by Gary Hardgrave, Minister for Citizenship and Multicultural Affairs, 23 May 2002.

3 As cited in George M. Fredrickson's *Racism: A Short History*, Scribe Publications, 2002, p. 119.

4 'Pay and Sex Yanked Diggers to Battle', the *Australian*, 26 November 2002.

5 As cited in Tim Flannery's 'Beautiful Lies', *Quarterly Essay*, Issue 9, Black Inc, 2003, p. 24.

6 'Comments Insult all Australians', editorial, the *Daily Telegraph*, 22 August 2001.

7 'Mafia Attack Alleged', the *Australian*, 15 July 1964.

8 Alphonse Gangitano was shot dead in January 1998. His suspected killer, Jason Moran, was shot dead in June 2003. The image of Gangitano wearing slicked black hair and Ray-bans is recycled almost every time the Melbourne gangland wars are covered in the media.

9 'Prisoners in Australia', ABS catalogue 4517.0, 30 June 2001.

10 Hunter S Thompson's *Fear and Loathing in America*, Bloomsbury, 2001, p. 185.

11 If the Lebanese pizza delivery boy, Sleek, from the SBS series 'Pizza' follows Nick Giannopoulos's footsteps to celebrity wogdom, then the Leb-lover should go mainstream in a decade from now.

12 As cited by the Victorian State Library in its pen portrait of Archbishop Mannix, www.statelibrary.vic.gov.au

13 John Howard's and Geoffrey Blainey's anti-Asian immigration comments are cited in Paul Kelly's *End of Certainty*, Allen & Unwin, 1994, pp. 124 and 423.

14 Pauline Hanson, House Hansard, 10 September 1996.

15 Greg Sheridan, 'I was wrong on Asians, says Howard', the *Australian*, 7 January 1996.

16 John Howard, interview with author, April 2002. The edited transcript that has been crosschecked by the prime minister's office

is on the *Australian's* website, www.theaustralian.com.au.

17 'Special report: Emigration', the *Economist*, 28 September–4 October 2002.

Chapter Two: Women and Work

1 Customised tables from unpublished census data, 1976, 1986, 1996, and 2001. Supplied to the *Australian* by the ABS.

2 'Work and Family Fact Sheet July 2002', Amanda Vanstone, Minister for Family and Community Services.

3 Calculations based on Housing Industry Association data, published in the *Australian*, 12 June 2003.

4 Customised tables from 2001 census supplied to the *Australian* by the ABS. The median incomes for computer professionals are $1045 a week for women versus $1187 for men; for GPs, $1118 versus $1316; and for nurses $786 versus $863 respectively.

5 The numbers on managers and administrators are from the published census.

6 John Howard, interview with Brisbane radio, 1 December 1999.

7 Family income data from unpublished census data supplied to the *Australian* by the ABS.

8 *Weekend Australian*, 14–15 September 2002.

9 'Births 2001', ABS catalogue 3301.0.

10 Don Watson, *Recollections of a Bleeding Heart*, Random House, 2002, p. 409.

11 Unpublished census data supplied to the *Australian* by the ABS.

12 ABS census, published tables for 1986 and 2001.

13 Customised tables from the National Centre for Economic Policy Modelling supplied to the *Australian*, May 2003.

14 Unpublished tables from the Melbourne Institute and Department of Family and Community Services HILDA survey supplied to the *Australian* August 2003. Sydney has 30.4 per cent of households paying off their homes in 2001 versus 36.2 per cent who have never been in the housing market. In Brisbane the figures are 34.7 per

cent against 36.1 per cent. All other capital cities have more home borrowers than those who have never held mortgages or owned outright.

15 Customised tables from unpublished census data, 1981, 1991, and 2001. Supplied to the *Australian* by the ABS.

Chapter Three: Sydney vs Melbourne

1 The ethnic mix of Bankstown, Marrickville, Mosman, Sunshine, Richmond, and Camberwell are from customised tables supplied to the *Australian* by the ABS. They draw on unpublished census material going back as far as 1954.

2 James Forrest, Kevin M Dunn, Ian H Burnley, and Amy McDonald, 'Everywhere Different: A Geography of Racism in Australia'. The survey was conducted between October–December 2001. The paper was delivered at the Institute of Australian Geographers' Conference in Canberra, July 2002.

3 As cited in Paul Kelly's *100 Years, The Australian Story*, Allen & Unwin/ABC Books, 2001, pp. 68 and 70.

4 'Births 2001', ABS catalogue 3301.0, table 2.6.

5 Data supplied to the *Australian* by the Department of Immigration, April 2002.

6 Calculations made by the ABS and supplied to the *Australian*. Note, the overseas-born and Australian-born figures used in this chapter may not add up to 100 per cent because in each census there are a small group who do not state where they came from.

7 Bob Carr and Steve Bracks, interviews with author, July 2002.

8 Media Monitors.

9 'Put to the test', Letter to the Editor, *Sydney Morning Herald*, 20 April 2002.

10 *Weekend Australian*, 26–27 April 2003.

11 Labor's federal vote in Victoria, after distribution of preferences, was 50.3 per cent in 1996; 53.53 per cent in 1998; and 52.14 per cent in 2001.

12 Tables supplied to the *Australian* by the Australian Taxation Office, August 2002.

13 Calculations use customised ABS tables supplied to the *Australian*, August 2002.

Chapter Four: The Economics of Motherhood

1 'Table 4: Higher Education Students by Age Group and Gender, 1980–2000', Australian Council for Educational Research.

2 ABS catalogue 3301.0, Births 2001.

3 2001 census, published and unpublished data.

4 Interview with Belinda Probert, July 2000.

5 John Howard, speech, Adelaide, 6 July 2003.

6 Customised ABS tables supplied to the *Australian*, January 2003.

7 Robert Menzies, *The Forgotten People*, May 1942.

8 Data and quotes from Ian Macfarlane speech, Canberra, 25 June 2002.

9 Ian Macfarlane, speech, Melbourne, 4 April 2002.

Chapter Five: Unfinished Business: the republic

1 All Newspoll figures can be downloaded from www.newspoll.com.au.

2 Peter Reith, interview with author, August 1999.

3 John Howard, press conference, Canberra, 23 March 1999.

4 John Howard, press conference, 8 November 1999.

5 John Howard, television interview, 10 August 2003.

6 Figures for Clayton Utz and Gilbert and Tobin were part of a survey released by High Court Justice Mary Gaudron in June 2002.

7 Unpublished Reserve Bank of Australia tables supplied to the *Australian*, June 2003.

8 ACTU research, 2002, leaked to the *Australian*.

9 Unpublished tables from the Melbourne Institute and Department of Family and Community Services HILDA survey supplied to the *Australian* in March 2003.

10 'The Rehame Report', 1995, 1996, 1997, and 1998.

11 The headline counts for Cheryl Kernot and Peter Reith relied on the Australian Parliament House online search facility, www.aph.gov.au

Chapter Six: Unfinished Business: reconciliation

1 The comparisons rely on published and unpublished census data for August 2001 and the ABS 'Prisoners in Australia', 4517.0, for 30 June 2001.

2 John Howard, interview with author, April 2002.

3 Interview with Keith Windschuttle published in the *Australian*, 3 September 2001.

4 Large towns are my term. The census adopts the misleading phrase 'outer urban areas'. What it is referring to is a settlement with a population of 1000 to 99,999. Most Australian Aboriginals are in large towns — 42 per cent; and 5 per cent of the total population of these areas.

5 ABS catalogue 3302.0, Deaths Australia, 2001.

6 John Howard, parliamentary question time, 4 April 2000.

7 John Howard, parliamentary question time, 6 April 2000.

8 John Howard, speech, Gallipoli, 25 April 2000. The numbers on World War I were downloaded at the time from the Defence Department website, www.defence.gov.au.

9 John Howard, press conference, Brisbane, 14 May 1999.

10 One Nation's membership was published by the *Australia/Israel Review*, July 1998.

11 Interview with Howard cabinet minister, December 2000. Note that all three ministers quoted in chapters six, seven, and eight were talking in the context of the day's events. Their views may have since changed for political or personal reasons.

12 John Howard, radio interview, Melbourne, 14 April 2000.

13 John Howard, radio interview, Sydney, 29 May 2000.

14 John Howard, radio interview, Sydney, 16 October 2000.

15 John Howard, speech, Canberra, 13 December 2000.

16 Paul Keating, speech, Redfern, 10 December 1992 (published in *Advancing Australia: the speeche sof Paul Keating, prime minister*, seelcted and edited by Mark Ryan, Big Picture Publications, 1995).

17 'Australian Candidate Study, 2001', principal researchers, Rachel Gibson, David Gow, Clive Bean, and Ian McAllister.

18 *Weekend Australian*, 3–4 August 2002.

Chapter Seven: Howard's Way

1 I joined the federal parliamentary press gallery in October 1988. The details of the Howard–Peacock rivalry that occurred before my time in Canberra have been fleshed out by Liberal contacts. I'm also relying on Paul Kelly's *End of Certainty* for specific events and quotes before my own corporate memory.

2 John Howard, speech to parliament, 23 August 1984.

3 John Howard, radio interview, Sydney, 8 October 2001.

4 John Howard, television interview, 17 February 2002.

5 Janette Howard, letter to Glenn Milne, 27 February 2002. She had issued a press statement a day earlier strongly refuting his original report.

6 'Australian Story', broadcast on the ABC, 16 September 2002.

7 John Howard, interview with author, April 2002.

8 Interview with cabinet minister, April 2002.

9 Interview with Howard critic, November 2001. Incidentally, the idea that Melbourne is the third-largest Greek-speaking city in the world after Athens and Thessaloniki is a myth. Chicago has long held that title.

10 Australian Gallup Polls, 1966. Supplied from archives by Roy Morgan Research, April 2003.

11 'Australian Candidate Study, 2001', principal researchers Rachel Gibson, David Gow, Clive Bean, and Ian McAllister.

12 John Howard, radio interview, Canberra, 3 June 1998.

13 The comments likening Pauline Hanson to Le Pen, and his

comment on the 1997 reconciliation speech, were also from the April 2002 interview.

Chapter Eight: The War on Boat People

1 As attributed in Anthony Summers' *The Arrogance of Power*, Phoenix Press, 2000. p. 294.

2 Where possible, I cite which party conducted the relevant polling. All of the material used in this chapter has been crosschecked with both sides, and against the 2001 census. To protect the confidentiality of various sources, I can't supply the titles and the precise dates of many of the polls.

3 Peter Beattie, election night press conference, 17 February 2001.

4 Interview with cabinet minister, June 2001.

5 John Howard, speech, Washington, 10 June 2002.

6 John Howard, press conference, 18 March 2001.

7 The Shane Stone memo was leaked to the *Bulletin* where it was published, 8 May 2001.

8 John Howard, press release, 27 August 2001.

9 Not all the Prime Minister's interviews are posted on his website, www.pm.gov.au. I've filled in the gaps with the additional transcripts that his office emails to journalists.

10 Figures are from the Department of Immigration.

11 The details of the Liberal focus group discussion were related in an interview in December 2002.

12 John Howard, interview with author, April 2002.

13 Kim Beazley, speech, 24 September 2002.

14 Lynton Crosby, speech, Canberra, 21 November 2001.

15 Australian Electoral Commission returns for the 2001 election supplied to the *Australian* in December 2002.

16 Customised 2001 census material supplied to the *Australian* by the ABS in December 2002.

17 Coalition ranks are strongest at the bottom — the home of Howard's battlers — where Liberals have 20 MPs and the

Nationals have twelve (for a total of 32); Labor has sixteen; and there are two independents. At the top, Liberals govern in their own right with 31 seats against Labor's eighteen and the Greens' one. The centre, as revealed in the introduction, was Labor's, with 30 out of fifty. The top ten seats are all Liberal: eight can be found in Sydney, the other two in Melbourne. The bottom six comprise four to the Nationals in New South Wales and two in Queensland, split between the coalition partners.

Postscript: Iraq

1 John Howard, address to the National Press Club, 13 March 2001.
2 Mike Steketee, 'Shocking Delay in Ending Refugees' Plight', the *Australian*, 29 July 2003.
3 Sources: Newspoll, UMR Research, and Australian Gallup Polls.
4 John Howard, press conference, Canberra, 3 February 2003.
5 John Howard, press conference, Canberra, 28 March 2003.
6 John Howard, Sydney radio, 30 January 2003.
7 John Howard, Sydney radio, 13 March 2003.
8 John Howard, address to the National Press Club, 13 March 2003.
9 'Haitians are Held in U.S. Despite Grant of Asylum', the *New York Times*, 25 July 2003.
10 The Newspolls on weapons of mass destruction were taken on 18–20 July 2003 and 31 January–2 February 2003.
11 John Howard, television interview, 14 March 2003.
12 John Howard, press conference, Canberra, 22 July 2003.
13 Newspoll conducted on 11–13 April 2003.